How To Be Alone Without Feeling Lonely

An Easy Guide to Enjoying Company with Yourself,

Growing Strong Mentally, and Surviving Rejection

Nicci Brochard
&
Dr. Ben Chuba

How To Be Alone Without Feeling Lonely

An Easy Guide to Enjoying Company with Yourself,

Growing Strong Mentally, and Surviving Rejection

CROSSBORDER

New York, London, Quebec

Contents

Introduction

Solitude has become humanity's forgotten superpower. Most people flee from quiet moments, filling every silence with notifications, conversations, or background noise. They mistake being alone for being abandoned, confusing solitude with isolation. This misunderstanding costs them one of life's most profound gifts: the ability to genuinely enjoy their own company.

The fear of loneliness drives countless decisions; staying in unfulfilling relationships, accepting toxic friendships, or desperately seeking validation from others. Meanwhile, rejection feels like a personal verdict on worthiness rather than simply information about compatibility. These patterns create cycles of dependency that leave people emotionally fragile and perpetually searching for external sources of happiness.

True strength emerges when you discover that solitude can be chosen rather than endured. The difference between loneliness and chosen solitude lies not in circumstance but in mindset. Loneliness whispers that something is missing; healthy solitude celebrates what is present. This book will teach you to cultivate that celebration.

Learning to enjoy your own company transforms everything. Relationships become choices rather than necessities. Rejection loses its sting when your self-worth doesn't depend on others' approval. Mental resilience grows stronger when you can retreat into your own peaceful space for restoration rather than seeking escape from yourself.

The pages ahead contain practical strategies, mindset shifts, and exercises designed to turn solitude into your sanctuary. You'll discover how to befriend your thoughts, find contentment in quiet moments, and build unshakeable confidence from within.

The journey from loneliness to self-companionship requires no special talents or perfect circumstances. Every tool you need already exists within you, waiting to be discovered and developed. Your most rewarding relationship—the one with yourself—is about to begin flourishing.

Nicci and I (Ben) thank you immensely for choosing our book. We promise you a great time ahead.

Chapter 1

Redefining Alone – From Loneliness to Solitude

Being alone often gets a bad reputation. Many of us have been conditioned to dread solitude, equating it with sadness or social failure. But what if being "alone" isn't something to fear at all? In this chapter, we'll explore how to redefine the experience of being by yourself – shifting the mindset from loneliness to empowering solitude. You'll learn the crucial difference between solitude and loneliness, confront the myths that make solo time seem shameful, discover the hidden strengths that grow when you enjoy your own company, and find practical ways to overcome the fear of missing out. By the end, you may start to see *alone time* not as a punishment or problem, but as a chosen opportunity for personal growth and mental strength.

Solitude vs. Loneliness – Understanding the Difference

Let's start with the basics: solitude and loneliness are not the same thing. Solitude simply means being by yourself. It's a state of physical or mental aloneness – for example, sitting alone in a quiet room or taking a solo walk in the park. Loneliness, on the other hand, is an emotional pain: a feeling of emptiness or sadness that comes from a perceived lack of connection. In other words, loneliness is not about how many people are around you; it's about how connected you feel. You could be in a crowd of friends and still feel lonely if you feel misunderstood or disconnected. Conversely, you might be completely by yourself yet feel perfectly content and *not* lonely at all.

To put it another way, being alone is a circumstance, while feeling lonely is a state of mind. One insightful discussion on this topic defined *"aloneness"* as *being content with yourself in the moment when you are by yourself,* whereas *"loneliness"* was described as a feeling of loss or lack when one is alone. The key distinction lies in your perception: Solitude is often a *chosen, positive state* – a chance to enjoy peace and reflect – whereas loneliness is usually an *unwanted, negative feeling* of being cut off or excluded. Simply being physically alone does not equate to being lonely, and realizing this is the first step in redefining what "alone" can mean for you.

It helps to remember that loneliness is fundamentally about feeling disconnected, not about physical isolation. This is why someone can even feel lonely in the middle of a party or a family gathering – if you feel unseen or out of tune with those around you, loneliness can creep in despite the crowd. On the flip side, solitude can be deeply fulfilling when it's *your choice*. Think of an artist absorbed in painting in a quiet studio, or a hiker sitting atop a mountain taking in the view. They're alone, but not lonely – they are engaged, present, and at peace in their own company. As one Psychology Today expert notes, *"while we think of loneliness as a negative emotional state, solitude can be a positive and enriching experience."* When you are comfortable with yourself, being alone becomes an opportunity to recharge and gain clarity, rather than a source of sadness.

Understanding this difference matters because it allows you to embrace solitude without fear. If you catch yourself conflating the two – for instance, thinking "I'm alone tonight, so I *must* end up feeling lonely" – challenge that assumption. Remind yourself that loneliness is not a guaranteed outcome of solitude. In fact, choosing to be alone at times can be empowering. It means you are *okay with yourself*, and you don't need other people constantly around to feel valued or engaged. Realizing that *solitude is a choice and loneliness is a feeling* puts you back in control. You can start to cultivate solitude on your own terms, using it as a positive tool rather than dreading it as an automatic source of pain.

Dispelling Myths and Stigmas About Being Alone

Even when we intellectually know that being alone isn't the same as being lonely, many of us still struggle with the stigma attached to spending time by ourselves. Society often sends the message that if you're alone, something is wrong. We've all heard (or had) those nagging thoughts: *"Why am I by myself on a Saturday night? Do people think I'm a loser?"* It's time to confront these kinds of negative self-talk head-on. In truth, there's nothing shameful about valuing your own company. Let's dispel some common myths about being alone and replace them with facts and healthier perspectives:

- **Myth:** "If I'm by myself, it means I have no friends or I must be a loser."

  Truth: Being alone does not mean that you're inadequate or that nobody likes you. There are countless reasons you might be alone at any given time, and none of them automatically imply a flaw in you. In fact, *choosing* to be alone sometimes is completely normal and healthy. Everyone – even outgoing, sociable people – needs some downtime. Remind yourself that solitude is a personal choice, not a verdict on your social worth. Often, people who enjoy solitude are perfectly capable of friendship and love; they're simply taking time to recharge or do something they enjoy on their own. Feeling content in your own company is a sign of self-sufficiency, not social failure. As author Emily White has observed, there is a "huge stigma attached to loneliness" in our society, which can make people erroneously assume that being alone is always bad. The reality is that *occasional aloneness is part of being human.* It doesn't label you as anything except independent.

- **Myth:** "Enjoying my own company is antisocial or means I'm depressed."

Truth: There's a big difference between pathological isolation and simply appreciating solitude. Choosing to spend Friday night unwinding by yourself is not the same as having antisocial personality disorder or being clinically depressed. Wanting alone time doesn't make you weird; it makes you human. One writer famously explained that for introverts, after socializing, *"to be alone with our thoughts is as restorative as sleeping, as nourishing as eating."* In their words, preferring a couple hours alone for every hour of socializing *"isn't antisocial. It isn't a sign of depression."* In other words, enjoying your own company can be a sign of psychological strength and self-awareness, not a character defect. It's perfectly fine to say, "I'm staying in tonight to recharge." That doesn't mean you hate people or that you're sad; it means you recognize your needs. Far from being a negative thing, this kind of self-care is healthy. By rejecting the false notion that loving solitude is "antisocial," you give yourself permission to meet your needs without guilt.

- **Myth:** "Needing solitude is not normal – I *should* want to be with others all the time."

Truth: It's a myth that constant socializing is the ideal and that wanting time alone is abnormal. Yes, humans are social creatures, but we are also individuals with inner lives. Needing occasional solitude is completely normal. Think about it: even the most extroverted people have moments when they crave a break – perhaps to think, to rest, or to engage in a solo hobby. There's nothing wrong with you for sometimes preferring your own space. Unfortunately, societal pressure can make us feel like we *always* have to be connected, responding, and available. We might worry that taking a step back means we're missing out (we'll address that FOMO soon) or that others will judge us. However, consider that being comfortable alone is actually a mark of emotional maturity. It shows you don't rely on others to entertain you 24/7 and that you can provide yourself with comfort and enjoyment. Remind yourself: wanting some "me time" doesn't mean you're strange – it means you value yourself enough to care for your mental wellbeing. It's *normal, healthy, and even wise* to take breaks from the social rush. There is no need to feel shame in saying "I need a quiet day to myself." In fact, doing so can make you a better friend or partner in the long run, because you return to others refreshed rather than burned out.

Challenging these myths takes conscious effort, especially if you've internalized them for years. Start by noticing the negative self-talk that arises when you're alone. If you catch yourself thinking something like, "People must be whispering about how I have no life," pause and counter that thought: *Everyone spends time alone sometimes; this is normal and even beneficial.* Replace self-criticism with self-compassion. Remind yourself of the truths above – that enjoying solitude is fine, even admirable. By systematically disputing the stigma and reframing solitude in a positive light, you gradually erase the false shame around being alone. There is truly no shame in it. As one article title aptly put it, "there's no shame in being alone" – the only danger is if persistent loneliness starts to impact your health or happiness, which we prevent by *choosing* and embracing solitude on our own terms. When you shed the myths, you'll see solitude for what it really is: not a problem, but a potentially enriching part of life.

Benefits of Solitude – Finding Strength in Aloneness

Once you start to move past the fear and stigma, you can begin to appreciate the real benefits of quality alone time. Far from being depressing, solitude can actually be *incredibly good for you*. Think of solitude as a fertile soil in which aspects of yourself can grow stronger – things like self-awareness, creativity, resilience, and independence. By spending time alone in a positive way, you give yourself a chance to recharge and develop a more robust sense of self. Let's explore some of the key benefits that come from embracing aloneness:

1. Self-Reflection and a Stronger Sense of Self: Solitude offers a priceless opportunity to get to know yourself better. When you're not caught up in others' company or external chatter, you can hear your own thoughts and feelings more clearly. In the quiet of alone time, you begin to discover your own likes, values, and identity on a deeper level. As one psychologist explains, when you connect to yourself in solitude, *"you can better know your likes and dislikes, connect to your desires, explore what you're interested in, and clearly know what you no longer want in your life."* This clarity empowers you, helping you let go of things that don't serve you and boosting your confidence in who you are. In essence, solitude is a mirror – it reflects *you* back to yourself. Regular moments of self-reflection can solidify your sense of identity. You might journal, meditate, or simply daydream, and in doing so notice patterns in your thoughts. Over time, you build a stronger internal compass guided by your own values rather than the noise of others' opinions. This strengthened self-understanding is one of the greatest gifts of being alone: you learn to like the person you are, and that self-knowledge becomes a foundation of mental strength.

2. Creativity and Clarity of Mind: Have you ever noticed how your best ideas often come to you in the shower, on a quiet walk, or during a solo drive? That's the power of solitude at work. When you're alone and free from distractions, your mind gets a chance to wander, and in that calm mental space, creativity flourishes. Research has found that people are more likely to experience "aha!" moments of insight when they are by themselves and relaxed. Without external noise or the need to socialize, your brain can think outside the box and make novel connections. Many great artists, writers, and innovators famously sought out solitude for this very reason – it gave them room to create. Moreover, solitude helps to quiet the busy mind and bring clarity. In everyday social life, we're often reacting to others or overloaded with information. But alone, you can process your thoughts thoroughly. Problems that felt tangled may suddenly unravel once you have some quiet to contemplate them. "Solitude helps us put things into perspective and gain clarity," one Psychology Today article notes. In that clarity, you may find solutions to dilemmas or a fresh perspective on something that's been bothering you. Whether it's brainstorming a work project or simply sorting out your personal priorities, solitude can be like hitting the mental "reset" button. The result is enhanced creativity, better problem-solving, and a clearer mind ready to tackle life.

3. Emotional Resilience and Independence: One of the most empowering benefits of spending time alone is that it can make you emotionally stronger and more self-reliant. How does this work? When you're alone, you learn to sit with your feelings – whether they're boredom, sadness, or contentment – without immediately running to others for comfort or validation. This builds your capacity to self-soothe and adapt. In fact, psychologists have found that solitude can increase your emotional resilience by encouraging self-reliance and healthy emotional regulation. Instead of always looking outward for someone to distract or reassure you, you become capable of handling your moods and challenges independently. For example, if you feel anxious, alone time might teach you to calm yourself through breathing or writing in a journal. If you feel sad, you might find that a solo walk in nature lifts your spirits. Each time you navigate an emotion on your own, you prove to yourself that you *can* survive it without immediate external help. This greatly increases your confidence in handling life's ups and downs. Along with resilience comes a profound sense of independence. Enjoying solitude shows you that you are sufficient company for yourself – you don't *need* others every minute to enjoy life. By embracing aloneness, you learn that you can fulfill many of your needs on your own, whether it's finding entertainment, comfort, or motivation. This realization is incredibly empowering: it frees you from excessive dependence on others' availability or approval. As one mental health resource puts it, spending time alone strengthens your confidence in your ability to handle life's challenges without constant support, cultivating an *"I've got this"* attitude. You start to trust yourself more. Then, when you do connect with others, it's out of choice and mutual enrichment, not desperation. In short, solitude can fortify your emotional backbone – making you both resilient in tough times and independent in your outlook.

4. Recharging and Stress Reduction: Modern life is noisy and hectic. We are bombarded by emails, messages, and the presence of people almost constantly. Solitude offers a much-needed sanctuary from this constant stimulation. Quality alone time allows you to recharge your mental and emotional batteries. Just as sleep rests your body, solitude rests your social mind. Taking even a short break to be alone can reduce stress and prevent burnout. For instance, a quiet evening by yourself after a busy week might leave you feeling notably refreshed by the next day. Many people find that solitude brings a sense of peace and grounding that counteracts daily anxiety. Without anyone else to worry about pleasing or responding to, you can truly relax. This is especially important if you're more on the introverted side – social interaction, while enjoyable, might drain your energy, so you gain energy back by being alone in a calm environment. But even extroverts benefit from occasional solitude as a way to *rest* and collect their thoughts. Think of alone time as an act of self-care: you're giving yourself permission to pause the hustle and simply be, without performance or pressure. In those moments of solitude, try engaging in soothing activities that you love – perhaps reading, taking a bath, listening to music, or just daydreaming. Such activities in solitude can lower your stress levels, improve your mood, and leave you recharged to socialize again later. By regularly retreating into solitude to recharge, you'll likely find yourself more patient, calm, and focused in all areas of life.

5. Personal Growth and Fulfillment: Finally, solitude can be a powerful catalyst for personal growth. When you are alone, you have the freedom to explore interests and thoughts that might get lost in a group setting. You can ask yourself honest questions: *Am I happy with where I am in life? What do I truly want?* You can set goals based on your own aspirations rather than on societal expectations. This self-driven reflection is fertile ground for growth. Without the constant influence of others' opinions, you might try new things that really appeal to you – starting a creative project, learning a skill, or simply thinking deeply about your values. Solitude creates a space where transformation can happen from within. Moreover, spending time alone intentionally can increase your mindfulness and self-awareness, which are key ingredients for personal development. By paying attention to your inner world during solitude, you might uncover habits or desires you weren't conscious of before. Many people find that in solitude they reconnect with passions or creativity they had set aside. Over time, this process helps you evolve into a more authentic and fulfilled version of yourself. Personal growth often requires introspection – and solitude provides exactly that. As one set of mental health experts note, time spent alone, free from distractions, allows you to "focus on your own growth" and make deliberate changes based on your own values and experiences. In other words, solitude gives you the clarity and space to grow. It turns alone time into an opportunity for continual self-improvement and self-discovery, which can be deeply satisfying and motivating.

All these benefits show that being alone can make you stronger, happier, and more creative – when it's approached with the right mindset. Solitude, in a very real sense, can nourish your mind and soul. Instead of fearing it, you can start to look forward to your solo moments as a time to recharge, reflect, and become the best version of you. Remember that balance is important: just as too little alone time can leave you frazzled, too much isolation can lead to genuine loneliness. The goal is to find *your* personal sweet spot – the amount of solitude that rejuvenates you and enriches your life, combined with healthy social connections. By embracing beneficial solitude, you'll cultivate inner strength that supports you even when you do face moments of loneliness or external challenges.

Overcoming Fear of Loneliness and FOMO

Even once you understand the value of solitude, you might still feel a twinge of anxiety when Friday night rolls around and you have no plans, or when you scroll through social media and see friends at an event you're not attending. Fear of loneliness and FOMO (the "fear of missing out") are very common feelings. We're social by nature, and nobody likes the idea of being left out or forgotten. The good news is that these fears can be managed and overcome with a shift in perspective and some conscious strategies. This section will provide a blend of practical tips and mindset shifts to help you handle those moments when being alone feels scary, or when you worry that you're missing all the fun by choosing solitude.

First, acknowledge that it's normal to occasionally fear being lonely or missing out. In fact, the urge to be included is hard-wired in us – psychologists note that early humans needed to stick with the group to survive, so our brains evolved to fear exclusion. In today's world, that survival threat isn't present, but our brain can still trick us into feeling anxious if we're not part of what others are doing. Social media amplifies this by creating a constant highlight reel of other people's parties, trips, and gatherings, which can make anyone feel like they're on the sidelines. So if you feel a pang of envy or worry seeing others together while you're alone, understand that *you're not alone in feeling that way.* Most people experience FOMO at times. The difference is that those who handle it well have learned to talk themselves through it and even turn it into something positive.

One key strategy is to remind yourself that your own needs and experiences are just as valid as any social outing. In other words, *prioritize self-care alongside social care.* If you are tired or just craving a quiet evening, it's completely okay to skip a social event – and you should not feel guilty about it. There is no shame in choosing "me time" over an invitation when that's what you truly need. Often we torment ourselves with the idea that we'll disappoint others or that people will judge us for not showing up. But consider this truth: unless it's a very crucial event (like a close friend's wedding or a once-in-a-lifetime farewell), nobody is going to be as upset about your absence as you imagine. As one writer wittily put it, *"The truth is, unless it's a wedding or funeral that you skipped, nobody really cares if you don't go to the party."* Your friends will carry on, and the event will be just fine. This isn't to say you should never socialize – of course maintaining connections is important – but it means you can let go of that excess guilt when you *do* opt out occasionally. The world will not end, and your true friends will understand. In fact, people are often more focused on having fun or dealing with their own lives than on scrutinizing who is or isn't present. Realizing this can be liberating. It allows you to make choices based on what's healthy for you, rather than out of people-pleasing or fear.

If the fear of missing out is biting at you – for example, you see photos of a gathering you skipped and start worrying you made the wrong choice – try a few of these techniques to cope:

- **Reframe the situation positively:** Instead of saying "I'm missing out on that fun," tell yourself "I'm choosing to invest this time in myself." Focus on what you *are* doing or gaining by being alone. Maybe you're finally getting a good night's rest, enjoying a movie you love, or simply relaxing without stress. Frame it as a *positive choice* for your well-being. This mental reframe turns the narrative from loss to self-care. Some people even talk about the "joy of missing out (JOMO)," which means finding happiness in the present moment you've chosen, rather than worrying about what else is happening. For instance, if you stay home to read a book and drink tea, savor that peaceful experience fully – that is your reward, and it's just as legitimate as anyone else's night out.

- **Limit triggering comparisons:** If social media is a major FOMO trigger for you, consider giving yourself a break from it, especially during times you plan to be alone. Remember that what people post online is usually a curated highlight reel – it doesn't show the whole reality. That party photo doesn't reveal that maybe half the guests left early or that the host was stressed. When you *do* see things that spark envy, keep perspective: every life has dull moments too, they're just not on Instagram. You can even deliberately detox from digital distractions during your solitude, so you're not tempted to constantly check what others are doing. Use that time to connect with yourself instead.

- **Gradually build your "alone confidence":** If being alone on a traditionally social night (like a Friday) scares you, take it as a chance to build your confidence step by step. Start by planning a small solo activity that you'll enjoy. It could be something as simple as ordering your favorite takeout and watching a movie you've been meaning to see, or working on a hobby. By *actively planning* a pleasant solo experience, you shift your focus from what you're not doing to what you *are* doing. The first time might feel odd, but notice that by the end of the evening, you're okay –

you might even feel refreshed. Prove to yourself in small doses that solitude can be enjoyable. Over time, these positive solo experiences add up and your fear of lonely Fridays will diminish. You'll remember, "Hey, last time I stayed in, I actually had a really nice night. I didn't miss anything earth-shattering, and I felt great the next day." This evidence quells the fear.

- **Value quality over quantity in social life:** It helps to remind yourself that having a fulfilling life isn't about being at *every* event, it's about appreciating the moments you do choose to have – whether alone or with others. You aren't going to look back and count the number of parties attended; you'll remember how you felt during experiences that mattered. Sometimes a quiet night of personal reflection can be just as meaningful as a loud night out. When you do go out, it will be because you genuinely want to, not because you're afraid of missing out. That mindset will likely make your social experiences more enjoyable because they're intentional. In short, give yourself permission to say "no" when you need rest and "yes" when you truly want to engage. Living this way – honoring both your social side and your solitary side – creates a healthier balance.

Finally, if the fear of loneliness itself troubles you (for example, worrying that you'll end up isolated forever), approach it with compassion and logic. Almost everyone feels lonely once in a while, and it's not a permanent state. Feeling lonely doesn't mean you *are* fundamentally alone or unlovable; it's often a signal that you value connection. Use that as motivation to nurture meaningful relationships, yes, but also to strengthen your relationship with yourself. When you are content with who you are, loneliness loses some of its sting because you know you always have *you*. Remind yourself of the truth: you are enough, even on your own. By spending time in solitude and developing your interests and resilience, you're actually making yourself *more* connected – connected to your own life and purpose, which in turn attracts healthier connections with others.

Think of building your tolerance for solitude like strengthening a muscle. At first, choosing to be alone when you're scared of missing out can feel uncomfortable, just as lifting a new weight at the gym does. But each time you face that fear and discover that everything turned out fine – you didn't "fall behind" in life by staying in, and perhaps you even gained something (rest, insight, self-respect) – you grow more confident. Gradually, the fear diminishes. You might even start to look forward to those self-chosen nights in, because you know they serve you well.

In summary, overcoming the fear of loneliness and FOMO is about rebalancing your perspective. It's about realizing that your life is not defined by an endless comparison with others' social calendars, but by the quality of your relationship with yourself and your chosen circle. By valuing your alone time as much as your together time, you send yourself a powerful message: *my well-being matters*. Ironically, when you give yourself permission to sometimes miss out, you often gain far more – peace of mind, energy, self-knowledge, and confidence. Over time, you'll find that being alone no longer automatically feels "lonely." Instead, it feels like an *option*: one that you can take when you need to care for yourself, without fear that life is passing you by. In fact, you'll see that life is very much happening in those quiet moments – growth, healing, and even joy are taking place within you.

By facing the fear of being alone and reframing it as chosen solitude, you take control away from FOMO and give it back to yourself. You are writing your own story, whether you're out with friends or enjoying a night of solo reflection. *You* decide what fulfills you. And when you decide to be with *yourself*, it's not a second choice or a consolation prize – it can be a deeply rewarding choice. Remember, you are never truly "missing out" when you are using time to care for and understand yourself. That is a rich experience no one can take away. As you practice this mindset, you'll likely discover a wonderful truth: being alone doesn't have to feel lonely at all. It can feel like strength, freedom, and the comfort of one's own company. That is the heart of redefining "alone."

Chapter 2

Embracing Solitude – Learning to Enjoy Your Own Company

Humans are naturally social creatures, but we also have a fundamental need for time by ourselves. In fact, some psychologists suggest that solitude is as basic a human need as relationships, and they view the capacity to be alone as a sign of healthy emotional development. Far from being a punishment or a problem, alone time can be a source of strength and calm. Research even shows that just 15 minutes of solitude can improve mood and mental well-being, helping to soothe strong emotions like anxiety. The key is learning how to embrace solitude rather than fearing it. This chapter will guide you in enjoying your own company. By cultivating self-awareness, engaging in solo activities you love, creating a cozy personal space, and unplugging from distractions, you can transform loneliness into positive solitude. Instead of feeling empty or isolated when alone, you'll start to feel content, recharged, and even empowered by your solitary moments. It's a skill you can develop with practice – and the rewards are well worth it.

Cultivating Self-Awareness and Self-Understanding

One of the greatest benefits of spending time alone is the opportunity to get to know *yourself* better. When you purposefully step away from others for a while, your focus naturally shifts inward. Without outside chatter or social pressures, you have the mental space to reflect on who you are, what you value, and what you really need in life. Consider using some of your alone time for journaling or quiet contemplation. For example, you might write in a journal about your day, your goals, or the feelings that bubble up when you're by yourself. Journaling is a powerful tool for self-discovery – seeing your thoughts on paper can bring clarity to what you truly want and what might be bothering you beneath the surface. Even simply sitting with your thoughts, without any distractions, can increase your self-awareness. It may feel odd at first, but try to observe your own mind: What topics do you keep thinking about? How do certain thoughts make you feel physically? This kind of mindful introspection is how you start recognizing your own patterns and preferences. As one expert on solitude explains, time alone gives you a chance to direct your attention to self-care and self-discovery, rather than focusing on other people. In solitude, you can finally listen to *your own* voice.

Knowing yourself is a tremendous advantage in life. When you understand your personal values, needs, and quirks, you can make choices that truly suit you – instead of living by other people's expectations or trying to fit into someone else's mold. For instance, perhaps you discover through reflection that you *need* a bit of quiet reading time each evening to feel balanced, or that you feel happiest working outdoors rather than in an office. With that self-knowledge, you can structure your life in a way that helps you function at your best. You become, in a sense, guided by an inner compass rather than the crowd. Psychologists refer to this as having a clear self-concept – a stable sense of who you are and what matters to you. Research shows that people with a clearer self-concept tend to experience less anxiety and make better decisions. They aren't easily thrown off course by others' opinions. In practical terms, this means that by getting to know yourself in solitude, you'll feel more confident saying *yes* to things that align with your needs and *no* to things that don't. As one Psychology Today article put it, people who enjoy their own company don't rely on others to define them or tell them what to do – they've built an internal reference for what feels right, and that's what they follow. The more you cultivate that inner understanding, the more solid and independent you become.

It's important to note that being alone might sometimes bring up difficult feelings – and that's normal. In the quiet of solitude, you might suddenly recall an unpleasant conversation or start worrying about the future. Our minds have a habit of replaying events and chattering away when external stimulation dies down. Rather than immediately trying to escape these thoughts, use alone time as a safe space to *process* them. Psychologists talk about engaging with your emotions with curiosity instead of judgment. If you feel sadness or anxiety arise when you're by yourself, try to gently explore it. Ask yourself, "Why might I be feeling this? Is there something in this emotion I need to address?" You might even write down what you're feeling or talk out loud since no one is around – whatever helps you vent or understand. By approaching your feelings in this accepting way, you practice self-regulation: you learn to soothe and counsel yourself, which releases stress over time. In other words, solitude can become a time to heal and decompress. Many people find that after they allow themselves a good cry or an honest think in private, they emerge feeling lighter and more in control. This process builds emotional strength. You prove to yourself that you can handle your feelings without immediately leaning on someone else to make you feel better. That emotional self-sufficiency is a rare and powerful trait – it means you're not at the mercy of others' availability or approval to be okay.

In summary, using your solo moments for self-reflection and honest introspection will steadily increase your self-understanding. You might discover talents or passions you had forgotten, recognize unhealthy situations you want to change, or identify what truly brings you joy. With more alone time, "you will be more self-aware" and can even course-correct your life toward greater happiness and satisfaction. Think of solitude as holding up a mirror to your own mind – at first you might notice only flaws or chaos, but with patience you'll also see your strengths, dreams, and authentic self-looking back. That self-awareness is the foundation for a fulfilling life.

Solo Activities That Bring You Joy

Solitude doesn't mean sitting in silence doing nothing (unless you want to!). In fact, one of the best ways to enjoy your own company is to engage in activities you love, alone. Rather than viewing alone time as something to "get through," you can turn it into quality time by filling it with fun, nourishing, or meaningful pursuits. Start thinking of solo activities as a menu of delightful options – things you *get* to do when you have time to yourself.

Consider hobbies and interests that you can dive into on your own. Reading is a classic solo activity that can transport you to other worlds and keep your mind happily engaged for hours. There's nothing quite like curling up with a great novel or a fascinating nonfiction book and a cup of tea, completely absorbed in the story. Psychologists note that getting lost in a good book can actually replace the urge to seek others' company – you're savoring the moment through the story instead of feeling an absence. Other creative hobbies are perfect for solitude as well: you might try crafting, such as knitting, scrapbooking, or painting, where you can express yourself freely. Or perhaps you enjoy playing a musical instrument, writing poetry, or taking photographs. When you immerse yourself in these kinds of activities, you enter a state of *flow* where time flies and you feel content on your own. People who are comfortable being alone often find great satisfaction and meaning in solitary pursuits – whether that's tending a garden, working on a DIY project, or exploring nature by themselves. They rarely feel bored when alone because they genuinely enjoy their own company while doing things they find interesting.

If you're not sure what solo activities you might enjoy, treat it as an experiment and give a few things a try. You could start a journal or personal blog to record your thoughts and daily reflections. You might discover that you love the process of writing once you start, and it becomes a cherished solo ritual. Or, try taking yourself on "artist dates" – a concept from creativity expert Julia Cameron – which means going out alone to places that inspire or delight you. For example, visit a museum or an art gallery on your own and take all the time you want to explore. Go for a hike or a walk in the park and really soak in the scenery at your own pace. Take yourself to a cozy café for breakfast or lunch with a favorite book or your notebook in hand. At first, being in public alone might feel a little awkward if you're used to having someone with you, but it can actually feel liberating. You get to choose exactly what *you* want to do, without worrying about anyone else's schedule or preferences. Treating yourself to a solo movie date or a nice meal out is a wonderful way to reinforce that your happiness does not depend on others' constant presence – you are fully capable of having a good time by yourself. In fact, many people come to relish these solo outings as indulgent "me time."

Physical activities can be fantastic solo adventures too. If you enjoy exercise, consider activities like running, cycling, or yoga done alone. A solo jog in the morning, for instance, can clear your mind and give you a rush of endorphins, setting a positive tone for your day. Going to a gym or an exercise class alone is also fine – you might even focus better on your workout without a buddy to chat with. Or try something meditative like yoga or tai chi at home, where you can center yourself and tune into your body. Exploring nature is another deeply rewarding solitary activity. Numerous people find that a solo walk in the woods or along the beach makes them feel peaceful and recharged; the quiet of nature coupled with gentle movement can be incredibly soothing. You might pack a simple picnic and go to a local park by yourself, just to enjoy the fresh air and watch the clouds or birds for a while. These moments of mindful solitude in nature can replace any loneliness with a sense of harmony with the world around you.

The idea is to fill your alone time with things that make you happy to be alive in that moment. If you catch yourself feeling the urge to call someone out of boredom, pause and consider: Is there an activity that sounds enjoyable right now that I could do on my own? Maybe it's re-reading a favorite book, baking cookies, playing a video game, or even organizing your space while listening to music. Have a list of go-to solo pleasures. Immersing yourself in such activities not only keeps loneliness at bay, but also helps you savor the present. One psychology writer observed that people who love their own company always seem to have something going on – they might be learning a new recipe, journaling, or watching a documentary that others would find boring – because they're genuinely curious and interested in life. This sense of curiosity turns solitude into a rich, purposeful experience rather than a void. You too can cultivate that mindset by finding *your* sources of joy.

Finally, remember that it's perfectly fine to enjoy leisure without anyone else. You don't always need a partner or friend to have fun. There's a special kind of contentment in realizing you can entertain and fulfill yourself. So next time you have a free evening or weekend, resist the reflex to scroll on your phone seeking plans. Instead, look at it as a chance to do something you love solo. Pull out that canvas and paint, blast your favorite music and dance around the living room, or plan a day trip to a nearby town just for the adventure. By making alone time fun and meaningful, you'll start looking forward to it. Rather than solitude being a cause for loneliness, it becomes a form of self-care and personal enrichment.

Creating a Comfortable Personal Space and Routine

Another key to enjoying your own company is to make your *environment* and daily routine supportive of solitude. If you craft a comfortable personal space – your own little sanctuary – and establish regular solo rituals, being alone will start to feel natural, safe, and even indulgent. Think of it this way: when you have a corner of the world that is set up exactly how *you* like it, spending time there by yourself can be a true pleasure.

Design your sanctuary: Consider setting aside a spot in your home that is dedicated to "you time." It doesn't have to be an entire room; even a small nook will do. For example, you might claim a cozy armchair by a window as your relaxation corner. Add a soft blanket or throw, some plush pillows, and perhaps a small side table for your mug of coffee or tea. You could decorate this space with a few items that bring you joy or calm – maybe your favorite books, some plants or flowers, warm lighting like fairy lights or a salt lamp, and personal mementos or artwork that inspire you. The idea is to create a *comfortable atmosphere* where you immediately feel at ease when you're there. One person described starting with just a corner in her living room: a comfy chair, a soft blanket, a few favorite books, and a small plant – it became her go-to spot for morning coffee and evening reading. You can do the same. Look around your living space and identify an area that you can transform (even temporarily each day) into a solitude zone. If possible, choose somewhere you can have a bit of privacy – perhaps your bedroom, or a quiet corner of the balcony, or even a section of the dining room with a screen or curtain.

Let family or housemates know that when you're in this spot, you're in your "me time" mode.

Outfitting your personal space might also include removing or reducing things that disrupt your sense of peace. For instance, consider making it a digital distraction-free zone. Our homes are filled with screens and beeping devices; separating your sanctuary from electronics can help signal that this is time to unwind. You could keep a charging station for your phone in a different room, so that when you retreat to your cozy corner, you're not automatically reaching for your phone or laptop. One article on creating spaces for alone time suggested setting up a "digital detox" spot – in other words, intentionally placing your electronics away from your solitude space. That way, when you're in your sanctuary, you're fully present with yourself, not half-engaged with the internet. Similarly, think about lighting and sound: using softer, warm lighting (like lamps or candles) in the evening can make your space feel more tranquil than harsh overhead lights. Maybe you'll play gentle background music or nature sounds if it helps you relax, or you might prefer silence. Noise-cancelling headphones or a white noise machine could be useful if you live with others and want to dull external noise. Tailor the space to whatever makes *you* feel comfortable and at peace.

Establish solo rituals: Once you have a pleasant space, integrate it into a routine that you look forward to. This could be a daily ritual or a weekly one (or both). For example, you might start each morning by spending 15–20 minutes alone in your special spot, sipping coffee or tea and perhaps writing in your journal or simply planning your day. Having a quiet morning ritual like this can set a calm, positive tone before the rush of the day begins. Alternatively, you might create an evening routine: maybe every night after dinner, you light a nice scented candle, do a few stretches, and then read for half an hour by yourself as a way to unwind. These little routines become comforting anchors in your day – times you know you will have to yourself, no matter what else is going on. Protect those times as non-negotiable appointments with yourself. If you share a household, communicate with your partner or family about your routine. For instance, let them know that from 9:30 to 10:00 pm is your relaxation and reading time, or Sunday mornings are for your solo walk in the park. Often, others will respect your routine if you explain that this alone time helps you recharge and will ultimately benefit everyone because you'll be in a better mood. Indeed, one study of adults who regularly sought solitude found that they would negotiate with family for time alone and found that *everyone* benefited when they got it – they came back to social time feeling recharged and ready to connect again.

Don't fall into the trap of feeling *guilty* for taking time for yourself. Setting aside regular alone time is an act of self-care, not selfishness. In our busy society, it's easy to think you must always be available to others or productive in tangible ways. But caring for your own mental and emotional well-being is just as important as caring for any other responsibility – in fact, it enables you to be your best self in other areas of life. As psychologists emphasize, self-care isn't just indulgent "me time," it's a crucial way to protect and sustain your mental health. Giving yourself permission to have a quiet cup of coffee in solitude, or to spend Saturday afternoon doing something you love alone, is healthy. It replenishes your energy and reduces stress, which means when you do engage with friends, family, or work, you can do so from a place of fullness rather than depletion. So try to establish at least a small window of solitude in your routine – even 20 minutes a day can clear the mind and nurture the heart. Over time, these moments with yourself will feel less like an unusual luxury and more like a natural, enjoyable part of your life. You may even find you start craving that daily sanctuary time because of how balanced and centered it makes you feel.

Lastly, don't be afraid to personalize your rituals. If you love structure, you might schedule different solo activities for different days (for example, Monday night is for writing letters or emails to reflect on the past week; Wednesday after work is for a long walk alone; Friday evening you treat yourself to a home spa night with a bath and music). If you prefer spontaneity, your routine could simply be a promise to yourself that you will spend a certain chunk of time alone, and you decide what to do in the moment. The consistency of doing *something* for yourself is what counts. By creating a supportive environment and routine for solitude, you train your brain and body to relax into alone time. It will begin to feel like when you step into that cozy corner or start that familiar ritual, "ah, this is my time to just be." That positive association is invaluable in helping you not feel lonely. Instead of emptiness, you'll feel solace and restoration.

Unplugging and Being Present with Yourself

In this modern age, one of the biggest obstacles to truly enjoying solitude is the constant presence of digital distractions. Think about it –

how often do you find yourself alone, yet immediately grabbing your phone to scroll through social media or text someone? Many of us reflexively turn to our devices the second there's a lull, filling every quiet moment with noise. While technology keeps us connected, it can also prevent us from connecting with *ourselves*. To fully embrace solitude, it's important to sometimes unplug and practice being present in your own company.

Try making it a habit to disconnect from digital devices during some of your alone time. For example, you might decide to take a daily walk without your phone (or put your phone on airplane mode and tuck it in your pocket just for emergencies). At home, you could set aside an hour in the evening where you intentionally turn off the TV, silence your phone, and stay offline. In those tech-free moments, challenge yourself to simply *be* with whatever is around you – and with your thoughts. Yes, it may feel uncomfortable at first. We're so used to instant entertainment and validation from our screens that pure silence or stillness can feel odd. But this discomfort is exactly why unplugging is so powerful: it trains you to find peace in *your own presence*. When you remove the constant pings and content streams, you allow your mind to slow down and process things. Creative ideas have room to bubble up. You might notice the beauty of little details that normally get overshadowed – like the pattern of raindrops on your window or the taste of your food when you're not simultaneously reading news on your phone.

A practical tip is to physically put your devices out of reach to avoid temptation. During your solo time, place your phone in a drawer in another room, or at least on a shelf across the room so you're not picking it up mindlessly. One psychologist advises that it's necessary to turn off devices on occasion: put your phone aside – out of arm's reach – and engage in the here and now. By doing this, you break the habit of using your phone as a crutch whenever you feel a twinge of boredom or loneliness. Instead, you give yourself the chance to experience the moment fully. For instance, if you're eating a meal alone, try doing it without any TV or phone distraction. Focus on the food – notice the flavors, textures, and aromas. You might be surprised at how much more you enjoy it and how calming a simple meal can be when you're present with it. Or if you're sitting in your backyard, resist the urge to scroll and instead watch the birds or feel the breeze on your skin. These grounding experiences remind you that *life is happening right now*, and you don't need an Instagram feed to make it interesting.

Of course, when we unplug and things get quiet, sometimes anxious or lonely thoughts creep in. This is normal, especially if you're used to constant stimulation. Rather than immediately texting someone for reassurance when you feel uneasy, try a grounding technique to center yourself in the present. One simple method is to engage your senses actively: look around and name five things you can see, four things you can hear, three things you can feel (like the fabric of your clothes or the floor under your feet), two things you can smell, and one thing you can taste. This classic mindfulness exercise can pull you out of swirling anxious thoughts and into the real world around you. You could also take a few slow, deep breaths and pay attention to each inhale and exhale – this helps to calm your nervous system. If you're on a walk and your mind starts racing with worries, consciously redirect your focus outward: notice the color of the sky, the architecture of houses you pass, or the sound of your footsteps on the ground. By anchoring yourself to the present sensory details, you interrupt the cycle of anxiety. As an expert in mindfulness, Jon Kabat-Zinn, describes it: mindfulness is "paying attention in a particular way: on purpose, in the present moment, and nonjudgmentally". The more you practice this while alone, the more you realize that your own company can indeed be peaceful and fulfilling.

If troublesome thoughts persist, remember that you have the power to manage them. When you're by yourself, you can actually talk yourself through an issue out loud or in your head, almost like you would comfort a friend. For instance, if you catch yourself thinking, "Nobody has called me today; I feel lonely," you might counter that thought with, "I may be alone right now, but that's okay – I can use this time to rest or do something I enjoy. I'll reach out to a friend later if I still want to." Turning negative, self-defeating thoughts into more compassionate ones is a skill that grows with practice. In solitude, try to observe when your mind starts spiraling ("mind chatter," as some call it) and gently guide it to calmer waters. One strategy is to keep a few positive or reassuring phrases handy – either written down or memorized – that you repeat to yourself if you start feeling down when alone. Examples might be: "I am enough," or "This quiet time is good for me," or "I am learning to enjoy my own company." By interrupting the anxious internal monologue, you reinforce that being alone is *not* an emergency; it's a normal, even healthy, part of life.

It's also worth noting that constantly checking social media can sometimes *increase* feelings of loneliness or FOMO (fear of missing out). Seeing others highlight reels can make you feel like you're the only one alone. Remind yourself that what you see online is curated and not the full picture of anyone's life. Everyone has alone moments; they just might not post about them. In fact, choosing to unplug and relish your solitude is something to be proud of – it's a sign of strength and independence. Over time, you may find that you don't even want to reach for your phone as much, because the peace you get from being present is more satisfying than the quick hit of dopamine from a notification. By reducing the constant noise of notifications and online input, you're giving your mind a chance to rest and reset. Instead of feeling lonely in the silence, you might feel a profound sense of calm.

In your journey to not feeling lonely when alone, learning to be present is perhaps the most transformative step. People who truly enjoy solitude often describe feeling very *grounded in the moment*. They notice little joys around them – how the sunlight falls across the floor, or how their hot coffee feels in their hands on a cold morning. They allow themselves to fully experience those moments without distraction. Their minds might wander (all minds do), but they've learned the "skill of returning" their attention gently back to the now when it drifts. You can cultivate this too. Next time you find yourself alone on a quiet evening, resist filling the space with noise. Perhaps step outside and gaze at the sky, or sit by your window. Engage with your surroundings or with one simple task and give it your wholehearted attention. In doing so, you'll likely discover that your own company is not lonely at all – it's actually quite rich. It's in those unplugged moments that you may feel a deeper connection with yourself and even with the world. As one psychotherapist noted, when people go within and connect with themselves, they often realize they are connected to the universe and all living things. That sense of connectedness can exist even in complete solitude.

In closing, embracing solitude is about building a friendly relationship with yourself. By cultivating self-awareness, indulging in solo activities that make you happy, creating a nurturing space and routine, and disconnecting from distractions to be present, you are essentially learning to *befriend* yourself. At first, being alone might have felt like being "unwanted" or missing out, but as you practice these strategies, you'll find loneliness giving way to contentment. You'll start to appreciate the quiet, to enjoy your independence, and to trust that you are enough on your own. This doesn't mean you don't need other people – of course, relationships remain important – but it means you're no longer fearful of solitude. You can be alone without feeling lonely. In fact, you might come to cherish your alone time as when you recharge, grow, and experience life most authentically. Embracing solitude is a lifelong skill and a gift to your mental well-being. So make that cup of tea, settle into your comfy chair, turn off the phone, and smile – *this* moment is yours, and you're in good company. Enjoy it.

Chapter 3

Building Mental Strength – Developing Resilience and Self-Compassion

Being alone does not have to feel lonely. In fact, alone time can become a source of strength and personal growth. Building mental strength means developing both resilience (the ability to bounce back from challenges) and self-compassion (the ability to treat yourself with kindness). In this chapter, we will explore how to do this through four key strategies: challenging negative self-talk, practicing self-compassion, growing confidence in your independence, and preparing coping strategies for the inevitable lonely moments. Each of these skills will help you enjoy your own company, feel emotionally stronger, and navigate any feelings of rejection or solitude with grace and confidence. The tone throughout is warm and encouraging, like a supportive coach guiding you to become mentally stronger and more self-assured.

Challenging Negative Self-Talk

One of the first hurdles to being alone without feeling lonely is confronting the inner critic – that nagging voice in your mind that tends to pipe up when you're by yourself. Perhaps you've experienced quiet moments that suddenly fill with harsh thoughts: *"No one cares about me,"* or *"I can't do this alone."* It's easy for such thoughts to snowball, each one making you feel more isolated. Psychologists note that this kind of negative self-talk only undermines your goal of finding fulfillment on your own. In other words, calling yourself a "loser" or convincing yourself you're unwanted will not help you enjoy solitude – it will do the opposite. These thoughts hurt because they feel true in the moment, but it's important to recognize them for what they are: reflections of fear or sadness, *not* objective facts.

Recognize the inner critic: The first step in challenging negative self-talk is simply noticing it. Pay attention to the script running in your head when you're alone. Are you judging yourself harshly or predicting failure before you've even tried? Remind yourself that just because you *think* something doesn't make it true. In fact, persistent negative self-dialogue can distort your perspective over time. Research shows that constantly putting yourself down can erode your self-esteem and even lead to feelings of isolation and loneliness. Knowing this, you can see why it's so important to intercept those thoughts before they drag you into a lonely spiral.

Counter false thoughts with truth: Once you've caught a negative thought, challenge it. Ask: *"Is this thought 100% true? What evidence do I have for it?"* Often you'll find the evidence is weak or non-existent – the inner critic is just being mean. For example, you might catch yourself thinking, *"I'm a failure; I mess everything up."* When this happens, pause and question it. Maybe you failed at one particular thing today, but that doesn't make *you* a failure as a person. You can replace that harsh inner comment with something more realistic and encouraging. In this case, you might tell yourself: *"I didn't succeed this time, but I learned something and I can try again."*

Reframing a thought from an absolute negative into a gentler, truthful statement robs it of its sting. Psychologists call this cognitive reframing, and it's a powerful tool. Instead of *"I can't do this alone,"* you might say, *"Being alone is challenging right now, but I'm learning and I will get better at it."* By actively rebutting the inner critic's exaggerations, you train your mind to adopt a more supportive tone.

Replace the negatives with a positive voice: After challenging a negative thought, consciously introduce a positive or compassionate one. Think of it as having your own back. You might keep a mental (or written) list of your good qualities and past achievements to draw on in these moments. For instance, remind yourself: *"I am strong enough to handle things on my own – I've done it before,"* or *"I am a caring friend and a talented cook,"* or whatever traits make you feel proud and worthwhile. These aren't empty platitudes; they are truths about you that your loneliness obscures. Research suggests that practicing positive self-talk in this way can improve your mental health and resilience. In fact, experts encourage using affirmations and focusing on your strengths to reinforce a more optimistic self-view. You might literally say to yourself, *"I am capable and lovable,"* as simple as it sounds. Over time, these kind messages start to feel more natural and can drown out the negative ones.

Crucially, stay upbeat about yourself when you're alone – this is a life skill that will pay off enormously. Dr. Simon Crisp, a psychology lecturer who has studied loneliness, says that *"being able to stay positive and upbeat about yourself when you're alone is a valuable life skill to learn"*. Without a personal cheer squad around, being your own cheerleader makes a huge difference. Adopting a "glass half-full" outlook about your life, even when no one else is around, will build emotional strength. According to Dr. Crisp, learning to see the good in yourself and your situation creates *"remarkable resilience"* that can carry you through tough times. In other words, by silencing the *"No one cares about me"* voice and amplifying a kinder one, you'll nurture a mental toughness. Little by little, you'll find that being alone doesn't shake your confidence so easily. Instead of feeling defeated by an empty evening, you'll tell that inner critic, *"I'm okay. I have myself, and that's enough."* This optimistic self-dialogue acts like an emotional cushion, protecting you from the sharp edges of loneliness and helping you bounce back stronger.

Practicing Self-Compassion

Loneliness often comes with self-judgment. When you hit a rough patch – say you're home alone on a Saturday and feeling down – it's easy to start blaming yourself for those lonely feelings. You might think, *"I shouldn't be sad. What's wrong with me?"* But berating yourself for being lonely only adds a second layer of suffering on top of the loneliness itself. A far healthier response is to practice self-compassion. In simple terms, self-compassion means treating yourself with the same kindness and understanding that you'd offer to a good friend. If a dear friend called you and said, *"I'm really lonely and upset,"* you probably wouldn't scold them or say they're weak for feeling that way. Not at all – you would listen, offer comfort, and maybe remind them of how much they mean to you. In alone times, you deserve that same gentle support from yourself.

So what does self-compassion look like when you're lonely or struggling? First, it involves acknowledging your feelings without judgment. It's okay to feel lonely; it's a natural human emotion. Tell yourself that. Instead of, *"I shouldn't feel like this,"* try saying, *"I do feel lonely right now, and that's alright – it's a feeling, not a fact about my worth."* This perspective – allowing the feeling rather than fighting it – is a form of kindness. Psychologists have noted that *"beating oneself up"* mentally doesn't prevent loneliness; in fact, it tends to make it worse. On the other hand, showing yourself compassion in moments of distress can be incredibly soothing. It's like wrapping a shivering person in a warm blanket. You acknowledge the cold, and then you offer warmth.

Give yourself permission to comfort yourself. When you sense that ache of loneliness or the sting of rejection, respond as you would to someone you love. This might mean speaking encouraging words aloud or in your mind: *"This is hard, but I'll get through it. I am worthy of love and care."* It might mean doing something gentle for yourself to ease the hurt. For example, fix yourself a favorite hot drink, play music that makes you feel peaceful, or take a long warm bath to relax. These small acts send a big message to your subconscious: *I care about my own well-being.* If your thoughts are racing with self-criticism (*"I shouldn't be alone, this is my fault"*), deliberately counter that with compassion: *"Anyone would feel lonely in this situation. I'm not flawed for feeling this way."* This kind of inner dialogue isn't about pity or making excuses – it's about understanding. You are essentially telling that sad part of yourself, *"I hear you. I'm here for you."*

Another aspect of self-compassion is remembering that you're not alone in your experiences. It's ironic – when we feel lonely, we often believe *"everyone else is happy, it's just me struggling."* But in truth, many people experience loneliness and self-doubt. Knowing this can help you feel more normal and less isolated in your pain. Psychologists call this the sense of *common humanity*. The fact that loneliness is part of the human condition means your feelings don't signify that you're broken; they signify that you're human. Remind yourself of that when you feel inadequate. *"It's okay that I feel this way. Others do too. It doesn't mean I'm unworthy – it means I'm human, and I need some care right now."* By validating your feelings in this way, you take away their shameful sting.

Self-compassion isn't just a nice idea – it has real benefits for your mental health. Studies have found that people who are self-compassionate tend to have greater life satisfaction, better mood, and overall emotional well-being. Interestingly, they also often maintain better social connections. Why might that be? When you treat yourself kindly, you nurture an inner sense of worth and security. You become less dependent on others to make you feel okay, which paradoxically can make your relationships richer (because you're not approaching friends or partners from a place of desperation or constant need). On the flip side, the *opposite* of self-compassion – harsh self-criticism – erodes your self-esteem and can even strain your relationships. If you're always internally telling yourself you're not good enough, it's hard to believe others could ever care about you, and you may withdraw or act defensively. In short, being gentle with yourself reduces feelings of unworthiness and opens you up to both giving and receiving love.

Practical ways to cultivate self-compassion during alone times include journaling and affirmations. Journaling allows you to express and validate your feelings on paper. You might write a letter to yourself as if you were a friend: *"Dear Me, I know you're feeling lonely tonight. I just want to remind you that you've been through a lot and you're really strong. It's okay to feel sad – anyone would in your shoes. Just remember, you are loved (by me!) and this feeling will pass."* Writing such kind words can feel odd at first, but it concretely shifts your mindset from judgment to kindness. Another technique is a simple self-compassion break: close your eyes, take a deep breath, and say to yourself, *"This is a moment of suffering. Suffering is part of life. May I be kind to myself in this moment."* This little script (adapted from renowned self-compassion researcher Dr. Kristin Neff) covers three aspects: mindfulness of your pain, common humanity, and setting an intention of kindness. It can truly defuse the intensity of loneliness by bringing a compassionate awareness to it.

Finally, think of developing self-compassion as building an internal support system. Life will always have ups and downs. Friends might not always be available, and external circumstances will sometimes leave you on your own. But if you have a strong habit of self-compassion, you carry an emotional safety net within you. You become able to catch yourself when you start to fall into despair. As one therapeutic guide on healing from abandonment puts it, *"Be attuned with your feelings, including sad ones, and use them as a spur to practice self-validation, self-compassion, self-acceptance, self-love."*. This means using moments of hurt as reminders to take care of yourself, not punish yourself. By treating your inner self gently, you send yourself the message that you matter and that you're not going to abandon yourself. Over time, this inner friendship greatly reduces feelings of loneliness or unworthiness. You realize that no matter what happens – even if someone rejects you or plans fall through – *you still have you*. You'll always treat yourself with respect and kindness, and that reliable support makes solitude much less daunting. In essence, self-compassion fills the void from the inside, so you genuinely enjoy your own company and feel emotionally stronger day by day.

Growing Confidence in Your Independence

Being alone can also be an opportunity to discover your own capabilities. One surefire way to stop feeling lonely when alone is to start feeling capable when alone. This section is all about building self-confidence by doing things *on your own* and realizing just how competent you really are. Think of it like this: every time you accomplish something solo – whether it's assembling a piece of IKEA furniture, cooking yourself a nice dinner, going to a restaurant by yourself, or even handling your personal finances – you are essentially saying to your brain, *"See? I can handle this. I am capable and self-reliant."* Those experiences, as small as they may seem, pile up as evidence of your independence. And evidence is hard for that inner critic to argue with! The more you prove to yourself that you can stand on your own two feet, the more your self-esteem and confidence will grow.

Start with small solo wins. If you've rarely done things alone, it can be intimidating to start. But you can begin with small steps. Maybe you take a solo walk in a new part of town, or try going to a café to enjoy a coffee without any company. At first, you might feel self-conscious –

that's normal. However, each time you push through that discomfort, it shrinks. You'll realize people aren't actually staring at you, and even if someone notices you're alone, it's not a bad thing. In fact, many people quietly admire someone who's comfortable doing things solo. By dipping your toe into independent experiences, you'll likely find them not only less scary than expected, but sometimes downright fun. You get to do *exactly* what you want, on your own schedule, without negotiating with anyone else's preferences. That sense of freedom is invigorating. Over time, you can challenge yourself with bigger solo adventures, like taking a day trip to a nearby city by yourself, or going to a concert alone because none of your friends like that band but *you* do. Each accomplishment, big or small, is like a brick in the foundation of your confidence.

One powerful effect of practicing independence is that you start to form a clearer sense of identity. When you're constantly surrounded by others, it's easy (often unconsciously) to let their opinions and desires shape what you do. Have you ever gone along with a group plan that you personally didn't love, just because everyone else wanted it? When you're on your own, that dynamic disappears – you have to decide what *you* want. This can be incredibly enlightening. You may discover, for example, that you actually love visiting museums alone because you can linger at the exhibits that fascinate you and skip those that don't, without feeling rushed. Or you might find that cooking a meal for yourself, exactly to your taste, is deeply satisfying in a way ordering takeout to please a crowd might not be. These solo experiences help you understand your own likes, dislikes, and values better. By focusing on your own interests without outside influence, you "get to know yourself" on a deeper level.

You begin to define who you are from the inside, rather than by others' input. *"When you purposefully separate yourself from others, you change the focus from them to you,"* explains one psychologist; this shift gives you the chance to truly figure out who you are and what you want out of life. In short, solitude can be a fertile ground for self-discovery and personal growth.

Dr. Simon Crisp emphasizes that enjoying your own company is crucial because *"you don't want to let others define you."* Instead, you can become the author of your own story. People who spend time alone and reflect on themselves often become clearer about their identity and values, which paradoxically can make them even more attractive social companions. *"The reality is,"* Dr. Crisp notes, *"we like those people who are really clear about who they are and [who] aren't constantly seeking reassurance".* This is a valuable insight: by learning to stand on your own, you develop a quiet confidence and authenticity that others respect. Think of someone you know who is very self-reliant – chances are, that person doesn't *need* others' approval to make decisions, and that independence probably inspires others around them. Knowing you can rely on yourself is a tremendous boost to your self-esteem. You stop seeing solitude as a void to be feared; instead, you start seeing it as *proof* of your competence and autonomy. For example, if you travel to another city alone and navigate everything successfully, you'll carry that pride with you. Later, if loneliness creeps in, you can recall, *"I managed that trip by myself – I'm capable of so much."* It reframes alone time as a stage on which you shine, rather than an empty space.

In practical terms, try deliberately doing certain tasks solo that you might usually ask for help with, just to see how it feels. Of course, there's nothing wrong with seeking help when you truly need it, but challenge yourself occasionally: assemble that new bookshelf without immediately calling a handy friend, or spend an afternoon hiking a trail alone (with safety precautions in place). Each of these independent ventures will teach you something about your own resourcefulness. You might surprise yourself ("I had no idea I could fix that sink leak on my own!") which naturally makes you feel proud and self-sufficient.

Spending time alone also frees you from the constant distractions or opinions of others, allowing you to fully immerse in your own experience. One article on mental health noted that doing things by yourself lets you enjoy activities at your own pace and in your own way, helping you avoid the pressures or influences that come from other people's input. This means you can be fully present and engaged in whatever you're doing, which often leads to better outcomes and more enjoyment. Whether it's working on a personal project or just relaxing, solitude can be a productivity and creativity booster because you have the mental space to concentrate without worrying about anyone else's judgment. In fact, research has shown that some people are happier and report greater life satisfaction when they regularly enjoy time alone. They often experience lower stress levels as well, likely because they've learned to be content with their own company.

As you accumulate these solo experiences, you create a positive feedback loop: each independent success makes you more confident, and with greater confidence, you're willing to try more things on your own. Over time, you truly grow into your independence. What once might have felt intimidating (like dining at a restaurant alone) becomes something you look forward to ("It's my treat to myself to have a peaceful lunch and read a book at the table"). One therapist observes that *"there is a greater sense of self that comes when you do things on your own – more confidence, [and] accepting of one's joys, limits, and passions."* Doing things solo empowers you to feel comfortable in your own skin, which in turn gives you a "much stronger feeling of self" and higher confidence. In essence, you're forging an identity as an independent person who is perfectly whole without constant companionship.

Keep in mind, embracing independence doesn't mean you don't need anyone ever – it just means you know you can cope on your own. That knowledge is incredibly liberating. It actually can improve your relationships with others too, because you're participating out of desire rather than need. You're no longer scared of being alone, so you can enjoy social time more freely and walk away when you need to recharge. The key point here is that solitude is not a weakness or a punishment, but a skill and even a gift. By growing more confident in your independence, you transform alone time from something that happens *to* you into something you actively use for your benefit. You become the hero of your own story, navigating life with the confidence that you are enough. As your independence and self-confidence flourish, loneliness will have much less of a hold on you – after all, how lonely can you feel when you truly appreciate your own capable company?

Coping Strategies for Lonely Moments

Even the most independent, positive person will occasionally feel a pang of loneliness. This is normal – lonely moments happen to everyone. Maybe it hits you on a quiet Sunday afternoon, or when you hear a sad song, or after you've said goodbye to friends and come home to an empty house. The goal of this chapter isn't to promise that you'll never feel lonely again; it's to equip you with tools so that when loneliness does strike, you know how to handle it in a healthy way. Think of it like having a personalized first-aid kit for your emotional bumps and bruises. If you prepare a "comfort plan" in advance, you won't dread those alone moments as much because you'll trust yourself to get through them.

As Dr. Crisp noted earlier, being able to maintain a positive mindset on your own makes you *far* more resilient when life throws challenges your way. In his words, the skill of staying upbeat about yourself while alone *"comes in handy during tough times – things like going through a break-up and dealing with illness"*. This resilience is partly built by knowing how to comfort yourself when you feel down. So let's outline some practical coping strategies for those times when you do feel lonely or upset. You can mix and match these techniques to create a comfort plan that works for you. The idea is to have a few go-to activities or habits that reliably help lift your mood or calm your mind. Here are some healthy, proven strategies to consider when loneliness creeps in:

- **Take a few deep breaths.** It sounds almost too simple, but slow, deep breathing is one of the fastest ways to steady your heart and ease anxious feelings. When you're lonely and your chest feels tight or your mind starts racing with negative thoughts, try this: inhale deeply through your nose for a count of 4, hold for 4, then exhale through your mouth for 4. Repeat this a few times. This kind of deep breathing activates your body's relaxation response. It's a mini form of mindfulness that pulls you out of your swirling thoughts and into the present moment. Even just 30 seconds of focused breathing can have a calming effect, making the lonely moment feel more manageable.

- **Get moving (even just a little).** Physical activity is a powerful antidote to sadness and stress. You don't need to run a marathon – the key is to get your body engaged in *some* movement. Stand up and stretch, take a brisk walk around the block, do a quick set of jumping jacks, or put on a song and dance around your living room. Exercise releases endorphins, those natural mood-lifting chemicals in the brain, which can help you feel better almost immediately. It also reduces the physical tension that often accompanies emotional distress. Research consistently shows that even light exercise, like a short walk, can improve your mood and reduce feelings of loneliness or depression. So when loneliness weighs on you, try to move your muscles – it helps shake off that heavy emotional state.

- **Do something creative or expressive.** Engaging in a creative outlet is an excellent way to channel loneliness into something meaningful. This could be anything: writing in a journal about how you feel, sketching or painting, playing a musical instrument, crafting, baking, or even just doodling on paper. The act of creating has a therapeutic effect – it allows you to express what's inside in a tangible form. For example, writing a poem or a song when you're lonely can release some of the ache in your heart onto the page. Even if you're not "good" at the activity, that's perfectly fine; this is about expression, not performance. The process itself can be calming and fulfilling. Mental health experts often include creative outlets in their list of healthy coping strategies, because expressive arts let you work through emotions and foster a sense of accomplishment. So pick up that guitar, grab some colored pencils, or knead some dough in the kitchen – whatever creative endeavor appeals to you – and pour yourself into it for a while. You may find that the loneliness fades into the background as you focus on making something.

- **Ground yourself in the present moment.** Loneliness often comes with a lot of past and future talk in our heads – *"I wish I had someone here right now... What if I'm always alone?"* These thoughts can spiral. A great technique to cut through that spiral is grounding yourself through mindfulness. One simple way to do this is to deliberately notice your surroundings and find something positive or neutral to describe. For instance, step outside and take a look at the sky, the trees, or anything in nature. You might say to yourself, *"The clouds are moving slowly across a pale blue sky,"* or *"Those trees look so beautiful in the sun."* Observing sensory details like this brings your mind back to *here and now*, instead of getting lost in worry. Dr. Crisp suggests this kind of exercise to his clients – when you catch your thoughts racing down a lonely or anxious path, refocus on the immediate environment. You could also try the classic "5-4-3-2-1" grounding technique: name 5 things you see, 4 things you hear, 3 things you feel (tactilely), 2 things you smell, and 1 thing you taste. This shifts your attention to your senses and away from the echo chamber of thoughts in your head. By grounding yourself, you interrupt the loneliness narrative and find a moment of peace in the present.

- **Reach out to someone who cares.** Just because you're learning to be content alone doesn't mean you should *never* seek support. Human connection is a basic need, and there's no shame in reaching out when you're feeling low. In fact, part of a healthy independence is knowing when to lean on your support network. Consider keeping a short list of a few friends or family members whom you can contact for a quick uplifting chat or even a text exchange. It might feel like you're bothering people, but think of how you would feel if a friend reached out to you in the same situation – you'd likely be more than happy to talk them through it. The same goes for your true friends. Sometimes hearing a familiar voice or receiving an encouraging message can instantly remind you that you're valued and loved, even if no one is physically with you at that moment. Mental health professionals note that talking with a friend is a perfectly valid coping skill. It can provide perspective, comfort, or just a distraction that makes the lonely moment pass. So don't hesitate to call your sibling, your best friend, or whomever you trust. You can say, *"Hey, I'm* *just feeling a bit down. Can we chat for a few minutes?"* Chances are they'll be glad you reached out.

Each of these strategies is like a tool in your toolbox. Different situations might call for different tools – sometimes you might need the quiet of deep breathing and mindfulness; other times you might need the energy jolt of exercise or the comfort of a friend's voice. By practicing these coping skills, you teach yourself that loneliness is *manageable*. It's not this terrifying void that overcomes you; it's a wave of feeling that you have the skills to surf until it subsides. And it *will* subside. Feelings are by nature temporary. Often, the fear of loneliness ("Oh no, I'm alone and I hate this feeling!") can make it feel worse. But when you have your comfort plan ready, you won't fear that feeling as much because you trust in your ability to care for yourself. You might even pin a list of your favorite coping strategies on your fridge or save it in your phone, so it's there as a friendly reminder whenever you need it.

One more thing: coping with lonely moments also involves a bit of positive self-talk (tying back to our first section). As you employ these strategies, tell yourself *why* you're doing them: because you deserve to feel better and this moment is not permanent. For example, while taking that walk you might think, *"I'm doing this to help myself feel better. This lonely feeling will pass, and I'll be okay."* Such reassurances actually strengthen your resilience. They reaffirm that *you* are on your own side. Over time, you truly come to believe that occasional loneliness is a part of life, but it passes and you have the power to help it pass more smoothly.

In summary, don't be afraid of lonely moments – prepare for them. With practiced coping skills, alone time becomes less intimidating and more empowering. Instead of dreading the possibility of feeling lonely, you'll carry confidence that if it happens, you know exactly what to do to support yourself. Many people find that this ability to self-soothe makes them feel *strong*. Dr. Crisp's insight bears repeating: those who learn to stay positive and resilient on their own tend to cope better with all of life's challenges. You become, in a sense, emotionally bulletproof. A breakup, a disappointment, a bad day at work – yes, these might hurt, but they won't break you. You've built up your mental muscles and your self-compassion, so you can face difficulties without collapsing. And when the storm passes, you'll still have *you*, standing strong and intact. That knowledge is the ultimate reward of building mental strength: you realize that you are never truly alone as long as you can trust and rely on the person you spend 24/7 with – yourself.

Being alone, then, transforms into a rich and even enjoyable experience. You have the resilience to weather the hard times and the self-compassion to nurture yourself through them. You have the confidence that comes from independence, and the optimism that comes from positive self-talk. With these skills, solitude becomes not something to fear, but something to cherish – a chance to recharge, to know yourself better, and to prove your own strength. So the next time you find yourself alone, take a deep breath and smile. You're in excellent company. You've got *you*. And you've learned that that is a pretty wonderful thing.

Chapter 4

Social Connections on Your Terms – Balancing Relationships and Solitude

L ife is a balancing act between the time we spend with others and the time we spend with ourselves. In Social Connections on Your Terms, we explore how to find the sweet spot between nurturing relationships and enjoying solitude. Everyone's ideal balance is different – and that's perfectly okay. This chapter will help you understand your own social needs, prioritize quality over quantity in your connections, set healthy boundaries to maintain independence, and discover how embracing solitude can actually improve your relationships. The tone here is conversational and uplifting, backed by expert insights and real-life examples to guide you toward feeling connected and comfortably independent.

Understanding Your Social Needs

Have you ever heard the term "social battery"? It's a friendly way to describe the energy you have for social interaction. Just as a phone battery drains with use, our social energy can get used up after a certain amount of interaction – and each person's battery size is different. Some of us feel recharged by spending time around people, while others recharge by being alone. Psychologists have long described personalities in terms of introverts and extroverts: introverts tend to gain energy from solitude, whereas extroverts feel energized by socializing. In reality, most people fall somewhere between these two extremes. *"We're all a mixture of introvert and extrovert – we need to know where our individual balance lies,"* says Dr. Simon Crisp, a psychology lecturer who studies personality and well-being. In other words, your social battery is unique to you, and understanding its capacity is key to a happy life.

Think of a day when you had a lot of social interaction – maybe a full day of meetings, a family gathering, or a party with friends. How did you feel afterward? Some readers might admit they felt buzzing with excitement, ready to keep the party going. Others might recall feeling drained and craving quiet. These reactions illustrate how differently our social batteries operate. There's no "right" amount of socializing that applies to everyone. One person might need daily chats and constant plans to feel their best, while another flourishes with just a couple of social activities per week and plenty of solo downtime.

Consider Alicia's story: Alicia is a friendly, outgoing nurse who genuinely enjoys people. She chats with patients and co-workers all day. But when she comes home in the evening, what she most looks forward to is an hour of peace and quiet with a book. At first, she felt guilty for turning down colleagues' invitations to go out after work, thinking "I must be getting antisocial." Eventually, Alicia realized that quiet hour was exactly what she needed to recharge for the next day. It didn't mean she didn't love her friends – it meant her social battery runs out after a long day of interaction, and recharging it with solitude makes her happier and more present when she does socialize.

Now contrast Alicia with Ben, a freelance graphic designer who works from home. Ben spends most of his day alone at his computer. By Friday, he's itching to get out and see people – he'll call up a friend to go to a trivia night or just wander to a local cafe where familiar faces are around. If Ben goes too many days without some face-to-face interaction, he starts feeling down and isolated. Being around others refuels him. His social battery works in the opposite way of Alicia's, and that's okay too.

These examples show how personal equilibrium can differ. The important thing is to reflect on your own needs. Ask yourself: *When do I feel happiest – after a lively gathering, or after a quiet evening? Do I often feel "peopled out" and need space, or do I feel lonely if I have too much time alone?* There's no wrong answer. By observing your moods and energy, you can determine how much connection versus solitude suits you best.

One useful exercise is to keep a simple journal for a week, noting your social activities and alone time. Record how you feel each day: energized, stressed, content, lonely? You might discover, for example, that two consecutive nights of going out is your limit and you need the third night to yourself. Or you may find the opposite – that a day without any social contact leaves you sluggish, and even a quick phone call to a friend can boost your spirits. Everyone's pattern will be unique. As you identify yours, validate it. It's *normal* if you don't thrive on the same schedule as your sibling or your coworker. Our society sometimes gives mixed messages – praising the social butterflies on one hand, yet also admiring those who are self-sufficient. The truth is, there's benefit in both traits. You might be more of an introvert at heart, preferring intimate chats or solo hobbies, or more extroverted, relishing group activities – but most of us blend the two. Embrace the mix that you are.

In fact, some experts refer to ambiverts – people who are equally comfortable being social or alone depending on the situation. Perhaps you've noticed this in yourself: you love going out on Saturday and laughing with friends, but by Sunday you're perfectly happy curled up alone with a movie. This flexible middle-ground is common. The key is to pay attention to your own "social thermostat". When you get the balance right, you'll know it because you'll feel contentment rather than either loneliness or burnout.

To illustrate the importance of finding the right balance, writer and introvert advocate Jonathan Rauch once humorously shared his personal formula. After observing his own feelings, Rauch concluded: *"My own formula is roughly two hours alone for every hour of socializing. This isn't antisocial. It isn't a sign of depression… For introverts, to be alone with our thoughts is just as restorative as sleeping, and as nourishing as eating. My motto? I'm okay, you're okay – in small doses."* Now, that ratio is specific to him – your ratio might be one-to-one, or five-to-one, or the reverse. The point is to find your personal equilibrium. If you identify with Rauch's need for plenty of solitude, honor that. If you feel more like a classic extrovert who's energized by people, that's great too – just remember even extroverts benefit from a little quiet time occasionally. There's no need to fit a label; just do what makes you happiest and healthiest.

By understanding your social needs without judgment, you set the stage for a more fulfilling life. You won't feel guilty for wanting a night in when everyone else is going out, and conversely, you won't feel "weird" for craving company when you've had too much alone time. Trust that whatever level of connection you need is valid. This self-awareness is empowering. When you know yourself, you can plan your life in a way that meets your needs – scheduling plans or solitude strategically – and you can communicate your preferences to others without apologizing for them.

Quality Over Quantity in Relationships

We live in an era of social media friend counts and networking events, where it can seem like *more* is better – more friends, more followers, more parties. But when it comes to meaningful relationships, quality matters so much more than quantity. Loneliness isn't prevented by the sheer number of people in your life; it's eased by the depth of connection you have with even a few people. In practical terms, having two or three close friends who truly "get you" can be far more fulfilling than having a contact list of a hundred people with whom conversations never go beyond small talk.

Think about a time you felt lonely. Was it when you were literally alone? Or was it perhaps when you were surrounded by people but felt unseen or misunderstood? It's very possible to feel lonely in a crowd. Imagine someone standing at a busy party, making superficial chitchat all evening – they might go home feeling emptier than someone who stayed home but had a heartfelt phone call with their one best friend. Real connection feeds the soul; surface-level interaction often doesn't.

Let's look at Marco's experience. Marco was popular in a sense – he had dozens of acquaintances through work and his recreational soccer league. His phone buzzed often with group chats and memes. Yet, when he went through a rough patch (his mother fell ill), Marco realized he felt very alone. He couldn't think of anyone in that big contact list whom he felt comfortable calling to talk about his fears and sadness. "I realized I had a lot of buddies, but no true confidants," he says. That wake-up call pushed Marco to invest more in a couple of friendships that showed potential for deeper trust. He grew closer with two people in particular – an old college friend and a colleague – regularly meeting for coffee and real conversation. Over time, those two became his go-to support system. Marco still enjoyed joking around with his soccer teammates, but now he also had friends he could be *real* with. The difference was night and day: knowing he had a few close allies made him feel supported and significantly less lonely, even though the total number of people he socialized with actually shrank.

Marco's story underlines a powerful truth: one genuine connection beats ten superficial ones. This isn't just feel-good advice; it's backed by research. A famous 80-year-long Harvard study on adult development found that the quality of one's relationships is one of the strongest predictors of happiness and even health. The study's lead, psychiatrist Robert Waldinger, has stated that it's not wealth or fame that keep people happy – it's feeling connected in *meaningful* relationships. In his words, *"Good relationships keep us happier and healthier."* Notice he said good relationships, not many relationships. You don't need to be a social butterfly; you just need a supportive circle, no matter how small.

It can actually be liberating to realize this. You can take the pressure off yourself to "keep up" socially. You don't have to force friendships or collect acquaintances to avoid loneliness. Instead, you can focus on nurturing the relationships that truly matter. If you have even one person you can call in the middle of the night when you're in trouble, or one friend who really listens (and you do the same for them), you are doing well. Those kinds of bonds act like a safety net beneath you – making alone time easier to enjoy because deep down, you know you're *not* truly alone in life. You have people who care about you.

Quality over quantity also means *shifting the way you socialize*. Rather than spreading yourself thin attending five different social events where you make polite talk, you might choose to spend that time more meaningfully with one or two people. For example, instead of going to a big group dinner where conversation stays on light topics, you might invite a close friend over for a long catch-up over coffee. Instead of trying to maintain connections with dozens of old classmates on Facebook, you might pick a couple who you really clicked with and give them a call or personal message. Depth requires attention and time, so choosing where to invest your social energy is important.

Here are a few tips for prioritizing quality in relationships:

- **Identify Your Inner Circle:** Think about who in your life you feel most at ease with – those you can share vulnerabilities or be your unfiltered self around. These may be family members, friends, or even a mentor. Make it a point to keep up with these people regularly. It could be as simple as a weekly text check-in or a monthly meetup. Consistency helps strengthen trust and understanding.

- **Be Present and Authentic:** When you do spend time with someone you value, give them your full attention. Put away your phone, ask them how they *really* are, and listen. Share your own thoughts honestly. Those genuine moments of presence create stronger bonds than frequent but distracted interactions. Quality time matters more than the number of hours; an uninterrupted half-hour heart-to-heart can mean more than a whole afternoon of half-engaged hanging out.

- **Let Go of Social Approval-Chasing:** Sometimes we pursue more and more connections to seek approval or avoid missing out. Remind yourself that *popularity is not the same as intimacy.* You might have fewer social engagements than some people you know, but if the ones you have are meaningful, you're in a good place. There's no award for having the most friends – the real "award" is feeling understood and appreciated for who you are.

By concentrating on quality relationships, you create a solid foundation that supports you even when you are alone. For instance, if you spend a lovely Sunday bonding with a close friend, you're likely to feel emotionally satisfied on Monday when you're by yourself at work or at home. The warmth of that meaningful connection carries over, acting like an emotional cushion. In contrast, if you spent Sunday hopping between three parties making small talk, you might find that by Monday you feel oddly hollow or disconnected, despite having been *around* people.

This goes to show, as the saying goes, "it's not the number of people around you that banishes loneliness, but the number of people who truly stand by you."

So, give yourself permission to keep your social circle small but mighty, if that suits you. Nurture those few friendships or family relationships that bring you joy and comfort. When you do venture into larger social settings, you might even feel more secure knowing you have genuine connections in your corner. And if you're a very social person by nature, that's fine too – you can still be the life of the party if you enjoy it! Just remember that at the end of the day, what counts is not how many attendees were at your party, but whether you went to bed feeling seen, heard, and supported by at least one of them.

Setting Boundaries and Maintaining Independence

One of the most empowering skills in balancing relationships and solitude is learning to set boundaries. Boundaries are those invisible lines that protect your well-being by defining what's okay for you and what isn't. They help you be with others *without losing yourself.* It might sound counterintuitive, but saying "no" or "not now" at times can actually improve your relationships in the long run. By setting boundaries and maintaining a sense of independence, you ensure that your time with others is enjoyable rather than draining or resentful.

Consider this scenario: Nina loves her friends dearly, but they are very spontaneous and always inviting her to last-minute outings. Nina is more of a planner and also values her weeknights to unwind alone. Initially, she felt obligated to say "yes" to every invite – after all, she didn't want to disappoint anyone or seem antisocial. Over time, however, she found herself exhausted and even secretly annoyed at her friends for "not giving her space," even though she never actually told them she needed some. The turning point came when Nina realized her friends weren't mind-readers. It was up to her to draw that line. So she started politely declining some invitations, saying things like, "Thanks, guys, but I'm going to have a quiet night in tonight. Have fun and let's catch up this weekend!" What she discovered was eye-opening: her true friends completely understood. In fact, some admitted they also appreciated a break now and then. By simply communicating her needs, Nina relieved the pressure on herself and eliminated the brewing resentment. She could recharge on the nights she stayed home, and then fully enjoy the outings she did join, because she wasn't running on empty.

Nina's case highlights how setting healthy boundaries is not about pushing people away; it's about taking care of yourself so you can show up fully when you are together. As researcher and author Brené Brown puts it, *"Daring to set boundaries is about having the courage to love ourselves, even when we risk disappointing others."* You have to value your own needs and time as much as you value those of your friends and family. This self-respect teaches others to respect you as well.

How can you start setting boundaries in your own life? Here are a few approachable ways to maintain your independence while staying connected:

- **Learn to Say "No" (Gracefully):** You don't have to attend every gathering or fulfill every request. If you're drained or simply craving some alone time, it's healthy to decline an invitation. You can be polite and appreciative: *"I really appreciate you thinking of me, but I'm going to pass this time. I've had a long week and need to recharge. Hope you all have fun!"* No need to invent excuses. A true friend will understand, and you'll feel relieved once you've said that honest "no" instead of saying "yes" and feeling miserable later.

- **Schedule Solitude:** In a busy family or a romantic relationship, personal space can easily get overlooked. Be proactive in carving out regular alone time. You might, for example, designate every Sunday morning as your "me time" to take a walk, write in a journal, or just sip coffee in peace. If you communicate this clearly (*"I need a little quiet time on Sunday mornings to myself; it helps me feel good for the week ahead"*), most partners or family members will accept it – they might even relish having their own time too! By putting solo time on the calendar, you normalize it as part of your routine, rather than something you have to beg for.

- **Set Digital Boundaries:** Constant connectivity can make us feel like we owe people instant responses. It's okay not to reply to texts or messages immediately if you're taking downtime. Consider letting close friends know that you sometimes turn your phone off or ignore social media for mental health reasons. For instance, *"If I don't answer in an evening, I'm probably just unplugging for a bit – nothing personal."* This sets the expectation that you're not always available, which is perfectly healthy.

- **Define Your Comfort Zones in Relationships:** Even in very close relationships, like with a spouse or best friend, it's important to maintain a sense of *self*. That could mean keeping up with hobbies that are just yours (say, you go to a pottery class Wednesday nights while your spouse has their game night – you each maintain individuality). It could also mean discussing boundary topics like how much time you need alone, or agreeing that it's fine to sometimes do things separately. For example, *"I'd like to go to the bookstore by myself for an hour. I enjoy that quiet browsing time. Let's meet up for lunch afterward!"* Communicating these needs prevents misunderstandings.

Setting boundaries might feel uncomfortable at first, especially if you're used to being a people-pleaser or if you fear conflict. But in practice, calmly stated boundaries often earn you more respect. People might actually admire that you take care of yourself. It also gives them permission to do the same. In a friend group, if even one person says, "I need a night off," others might sigh with relief and say, "You know, me too!" It only takes one brave soul to normalize listening to our own limits.

Maintaining independence doesn't mean being isolated; it means preserving your sense of self while you engage with others. Think of it like keeping one foot on solid ground while the other steps into social life. For instance, if you're in a romantic relationship, you can be deeply connected yet still your own person. In fact, healthy relationships thrive when both individuals have a strong sense of self. It prevents the relationship from becoming claustrophobic. You'll have more to talk about when each of you is pursuing your own interests in addition to your shared activities.

Also, setting boundaries helps prevent burnout and resentment. When you continually override your own needs to please others, you build up stress and quiet frustration. Over time, that can leak out as irritability or resentment toward the very people you care about. By contrast, when you honor your need for space or rest, you refill your patience and love. You're then able to be a better friend/partner/parent when you do connect with people, because you're not running on fumes or feeling like a martyr.

Dr. Simon Crisp notes that modern life can create a "social treadmill" – we sometimes feel we have to keep up with every social event and message, or else we'll fall behind or disappoint someone. But constantly running on that treadmill isn't sustainable. *The solution?* As Dr. Crisp suggests, value your own needs and time as much as those of your mates. That might mean choosing to stay home when you're sick or exhausted, even if there's a big event (there will be other parties, after all). It could mean going to bed early on a Friday night because that's what your body and mind crave, despite any Fear of Missing Out. The world will not end if you skip an outing – in fact, you might feel so much better the next day that when you do meet your friends, you're in a great mood, ready to engage wholeheartedly. By asserting these small boundaries, you teach others that you respect yourself, and interestingly, it often raises their respect for you too. You become known as someone who is confident enough to take care of themselves.

In summary, independence and connection are not mutually exclusive. You can be a loyal friend or loving family member and still say "no" when you need to, still take time just for you. Those who matter will understand. And those who don't understand probably don't respect personal boundaries – which is an issue with them, not you. Protect your mental and emotional space, and you'll find your relationships become more balanced and stress-free.

When Solitude Enriches Relationships

It might surprise you, but one of the best ways to improve your relationships with others is to improve the relationship you have *with yourself*. When you are comfortable on your own, you bring a stronger, healthier version of yourself into your social interactions. Think of solitude and companionship as two sides of the same coin rather than opposing forces. The confidence and peace you cultivate while alone can spill over positively into how you connect with friends, family, and partners.

Picture someone who has not learned to be alone – they might become clingy or dependent in friendships or romance because they constantly need reassurance that they are valued. Now picture someone who enjoys their own company – they are likely to approach relationships from a place of security rather than neediness. Which person do you imagine is easier to be around? Most of us would prefer the company of someone who isn't anxiously hanging on our every move, and instead brings positive energy into the room. By being content with yourself, you inadvertently make others more content with you as well.

Priya's journey is a great example of this paradox. Priya used to panic at the thought of being alone. In her early twenties, she jumped from one relationship to the next and filled every weekend with social engagements. She was afraid that if she slowed down, she'd feel lonely or "left out." Over time, though, Priya noticed a pattern: her fear of loneliness was actually making her relationships strained. She often felt anxious if her boyfriend wanted a night out with his buddies (without her), or she'd get upset if a friend didn't invite her to some outing — interpreting it as a personal rejection. This led to arguments and drama that pushed people away. After a particularly painful breakup, Priya decided to try a different approach. She consciously took a few months *off* from dating and cut back on her social calendar to get to know herself better. It wasn't easy at first — she felt the itch to text people or seek company — but she started small: a solo movie here, a cafe lunch by herself there, gradually building up her confidence being alone. She also picked up activities she realized she loved, like painting and evening jogs, which she'd never made time for before. As the weeks passed, something shifted: Priya began to genuinely enjoy her own presence. She found a sense of calm in her routine of morning jogs and painting on Saturday afternoons. Her thoughts during alone time became less harsh and more comforting as she practiced encouraging herself instead of criticizing.

When Priya re-engaged with her social life, her friends noticed the change. She seemed more at ease and wasn't as reactive. If someone canceled plans, she took it in stride (after all, she had plenty of ways to enjoy an unexpected free evening). When she eventually started dating someone new, she didn't feel the old urge to spend every waking moment together. She was fine if they each did their own thing some days. This new relationship blossomed much more smoothly. Her newfound self-sufficiency allowed love to breathe – there was space for both partners to be themselves, and they appreciated each other's company more knowing it was by choice, not desperation. Priya reflected, "I used to think being alone was the worst thing. But once I got comfortable with it, I became less worried and jealous in relationships. I know I'll be okay on my own, so I'm not clinging anymore. Ironically, that has brought me closer to people."

Priya's story shows how solitude can enrich relationships rather than threaten them. By enjoying time alone, you reduce the pressure you might unconsciously place on friends or partners to "complete" you or entertain you constantly. You approach them as a whole person, not a half in search of another half. That mindset is attractive and reassuring to others. Your friends will sense that you *want* their company but don't *need* it like a lifeline – and that actually makes them often more eager to be with you, because it feels free and positive.

Experts reinforce this idea. Dr. Simon Crisp points out that *being comfortable in your own skin makes your relationships better because you'll be a calmer, more grounded person.* When you're not constantly seeking validation from others, you can interact more genuinely and patiently. You might listen more when your friend is venting, instead of anxiously waiting for them to reassure you about something. You might give your partner the benefit of the doubt, instead of overthinking every small silence or text delay as a sign of rejection. In short, you show up as a secure individual, which creates a safe space for others to relax and connect with you. People appreciate this confident, easygoing presence – it's magnetic in a quiet way.

There's a saying: *"You must love yourself before you can truly love others."* Loving yourself in this context partly means enjoying your own company and valuing yourself enough not to lose self-respect in relationships. When you have that self-love, you set a tone in relationships that says, "I am happy being me, and I'm happy you're in my life too." It removes a lot of unspoken burden. Your loved ones don't feel responsible for your constant happiness – which is a relief because, truthfully, no one can bear that responsibility for someone else 24/7. Instead, they get to share happiness *with* you, which is much more enjoyable.

Solitude can also give you new insights and energy that benefit your relationships. When you spend time alone reflecting, learning, or simply resting, you often come back to your social world with more to give. Maybe during a solo hike you processed some stress and now you're less tense when you meet your family. Or you picked up a new skill or read an interesting book in your alone time, and now you have fresh ideas and stories to share with friends. Alone time can be profoundly creative and nourishing – many artists, writers, and thinkers have cherished solitude for this reason. You don't have to be an artist to reap the benefits; even journaling your thoughts or daydreaming on your own can lead to personal growth. And when we grow individually, we often bring those growth gifts into our relationships.

For example, imagine Leo, who started practicing meditation during his solitary mornings. This personal habit taught him how to calm his racing thoughts. When conflicts or misunderstandings arose with his friends later, Leo found he was less reactive – he could pause, take a breath, and respond more thoughtfully. His friends commented on how patient and wise he seemed lately. Leo credits that to the self-work he did when he was alone. His solitude indirectly made him a better friend, someone who could lend a calm perspective or just not add fuel to the fire during tense times.

Another way solitude enriches relationships is by preventing codependency. Codependency is a pattern where someone's sense of worth and mood become overly tied to another person, often leading to controlling or people-pleasing behaviors. Spending time alone building up your own happiness acts as a safeguard against that. You realize you are capable of being okay on your own, which means you don't have to latch onto someone else for dear life. Instead of thinking "I'd be nothing without my friends/partner," you think "I'm something all by myself, and having friends/partner is a wonderful bonus." This mindset actually fosters healthier interdependence: you support each other but aren't entangled or suffocating one another.

It's important to note that solitude and companionship are not opposing forces; they complement each other when balanced. Too much socializing with zero alone time can leave a person exhausted and irritable – not exactly a recipe for being a good friend or partner. On the flip side, too much isolation without any support can make a person overly anxious or out of touch when they do try to connect. The magic happens in the middle. Solitude gives you the chance to recharge and know yourself; connection gives you the chance to bond and grow with others. Each one enhances the other. When you've had enriching alone time, you often feel excited to see friends and genuinely interested in them because your own cup is full. After a great time with loved ones, solitude can feel even sweeter – a quiet space to savor memories and regroup your energy.

Consider solitude as the time when you charge your batteries, and social time as when you shine that energy outward. If you charge too little, the light you bring to others might dim. If you never go out and shine, you miss out on the joy of shared light. Balance means you regularly charge *and* regularly shine. And if you maintain that balance on *your terms*, you won't feel lonely when alone, nor overwhelmed when with others. You'll simply feel in control of your life and satisfied with the mix of experiences.

To wrap up, being alone without feeling lonely is an art – and part of that art is knowing that your alone time actually serves your relationships. The stronger and more content you become in yourself, the more you have to offer in friendship and love. Dr. Crisp emphasizes that feeling good inside yourself translates into being patient, confident, and positive around others – qualities that naturally attract people and deepen bonds. By now, you can see the beautiful irony: when you cherish your solitude, you often enhance your sense of connection with the world. You carry an inner assurance that you are never truly alone because *you* are there for you. And with that assurance, you can engage with others in a wholehearted, relaxed way.

In conclusion, balancing relationships and solitude is a highly personal journey. Understanding your unique social needs helps you strike a comfortable balance. Prioritizing quality connections over sheer quantity ensures you have real support and love in your life. Setting boundaries and maintaining independence protect your energy and identity, which in turn improves how you relate to others. And embracing solitude as a positive force can actually deepen your relationships by making you a more secure and compassionate companion. Remember, there's no universal formula – but by listening to yourself and honoring both your need for others and your need for yourself, you can create a life where being alone doesn't equal feeling lonely. Instead, alone time becomes a source of strength and joy that complements your social time. You truly can have the best of both worlds: the fulfilling company of others and the peaceful company of yourself.

Chapter 5

Growing and Thriving in Solitude – Turning Alone Time into Personal Growth

Solitude often gets a bad rap in our hyper-connected world, but spending time alone doesn't have to mean feeling lonely. In fact, it can be an opportunity and a gift. As writer Laurence Sterne once observed, *"In solitude, the mind gains strength and learns to lean upon itself."* Far from being a social failure, choosing to be alone at times is a way to reconnect with yourself. Research reveals that intentional time alone can actually reduce stress, spark creativity, and improve emotional health. Think about it – when you're by yourself, free from notifications and others' expectations, you have the mental space to explore what you truly enjoy and to grow stronger mentally. In this chapter, we'll dive into how to turn that *alone time* into periods of personal growth. We'll cover finding passion projects that excite you, tapping into creativity during quiet moments, working on self-improvement goals, and even celebrating big solo adventures. By the end, you'll see how being alone can be fulfilling – even empowering – rather than lonely.

Finding Your Passion Projects

One of the best ways to make solitude rewarding is to dive into passion projects – the hobbies and interests that light you up. When you're alone, free from others' opinions or expectations, you have permission to explore anything that truly excites you. Solitude strips away external influences, revealing your *true* interests and passions. Think of it as a chance to ask yourself: *What would I love to do if nobody could judge me for it?* Without an audience, you might discover a latent passion for something you never gave yourself time for before.

Now is the time to dust off those old hobbies or try brand new ones. Have you always wanted to write a novel or a blog? Start journaling your thoughts or drafting stories. Maybe you used to play guitar or piano years ago – pick it up again and see where the music takes you. Is there an online course you saved but never started on coding, photography, or a foreign language? Dive in at your own pace. Perhaps you've dreamed of cooking elaborate recipes from French pastries to homemade pasta; go ahead and turn your kitchen into a solo cooking adventure. The beauty of passion projects in solitude is that you set the rules. There's no one around to criticize or rush you. You can spend a whole Sunday tinkering with a DIY craft, learning to code a simple app, painting an amateur canvas, or tending a balcony garden – whatever brings you joy and a sense of curiosity.

Pursuing these personal projects gives a powerful sense of *purpose* and *joy* that transforms alone time into something rewarding rather than isolating. In fact, research backs this up: a large 2023 study of about 93,000 people found that those who had hobbies reported better health, more happiness, and higher life satisfaction than those who didn't. Hobbies often involve creativity, self-expression, relaxation, and even a bit of challenge – all ingredients for good mental health. So if you receive the occasional tease like "Why are you knitting by yourself?" or "Why spend hours baking with no one to eat it?", remember that these activities are far from trivial – they're keeping you mentally and emotionally healthy, and making your alone time something you look forward to.

It can be inspiring to realize that many personal passions are discovered in solitude. Free from the pressure to "fit in" with what friends or family like, you might stumble on an interest that truly feels like *you*. For example, one student writer, reflecting on finding her calling, put it this way: *"If our lives are so small and unique to us, why not use the time to do what you want? Your passion is yours alone—don't forget that!"*. This is terrific advice. Your alone time is your time – a chance to delve into whatever fascinates you without worrying whether it's cool or productive enough for someone else. Whether it's writing fan-fiction, learning magic tricks, or researching genealogy, no interest is too silly if it gives you that spark of excitement.

And don't be afraid to experiment. Maybe you try watercolor painting in your quiet hours and realize it isn't your thing – that's okay! Solitude is a safe testing ground. You can move on to another project until you feel that click of passion. Many people end up discovering lifelong interests when they're alone. The famous scientist Isaac Newton, for instance, made some of his greatest breakthroughs while working in solitude during a pandemic quarantine. You never know what *you* might discover or create when you give yourself permission to explore. The key is to approach your passion projects with a sense of play and openness. Set aside a slice of your alone time for these activities, and protect it as a date with yourself. Over time, you'll start to cherish these solo creative sessions. Instead of dreading being alone, you'll find yourself saying "I finally get to work on my novel!" or "Great, tonight I can experiment with new recipes." Your hobbies and projects will become companions that make solitude sweet.

Most importantly, celebrate the joy these passion projects bring. Savor the fact that you're doing something *just for you*. Finishing a personal project – whether it's a short story, a knitted scarf, or a small home improvement – can give a deep sense of accomplishment. You did it on your own, for your own fulfillment, and that feeling is incredibly satisfying. Alone time spent this way becomes inherently meaningful. Instead of feeling empty, your solo hours are filled with purpose and creativity. By finding your passion projects and nurturing them, you transform solitude from a void into a creative haven.

Creativity and Inspiration in Quiet Moments

Have you ever noticed how your best ideas often pop up when you're alone and relaxed – maybe while taking a peaceful walk or even in the shower? It's not a coincidence. Solitude can be a *wellspring of creativity*. When you're not surrounded by noise and chatter, your mind is freer to wander and make novel connections. Albert Einstein famously said, *"The monotony and solitude of a quiet life stimulates the creative mind."* Indeed, science agrees that a bit of quiet alone time can ignite your imagination. Studies suggest that many creative breakthroughs happen during moments of uninterrupted thought, when your brain is allowed to daydream without distractions. In fact, psychologists have found that those sudden *"aha!"* insights – the eureka moments – usually strike when our minds are relatively calm and we're not actively trying to force the solution. Silence and solitude are critical for these moments of inspiration.

Think about it: when you're alone, you can let your mind play. You might start pondering a problem or imagining a scenario, and without external input, your thoughts can roam in original directions. Daydreaming, which we often dismiss as "wasting time," is actually a powerful creative tool. One Psychology Today article notes that *stepping away* from a task and allowing your mind to wander freely can lead to new ideas and creative insights by engaging unconscious thought processes. Ever had the experience of struggling with a challenge, only to have the perfect idea hit you while you were taking a solo drive or washing dishes alone? That's your quiet mind at work. A bit of solitude encourages these fertile mental meanderings. As one writer quipped, cherish those quiet moments – even something as simple as sitting by a window with your thoughts can spark inspiration.

To make the most of these creative sparks, embrace the quiet times instead of rushing through them. For instance, you might keep a sketchpad or notebook handy during your solitary moments. Go for an aimless stroll in the park, sit on a bench, and just observe the world – let your thoughts flow and see what ideas bubble up. If you're at home, maybe set aside 10 minutes to close your eyes and daydream or meditate on a question. Some people find their minds are especially inventive during routine solo activities like morning showers or evening jogs.

Rather than distracting yourself with music or podcasts *every* time, try occasionally showering in silence or jogging without earbuds, giving your imagination room to play. You might be surprised by the *"lightbulb"* ideas that appear.

Remember, creativity isn't only for artists or writers – it can be about problem-solving in daily life, brainstorming business ideas, or simply thinking of fun plans for the weekend. By framing alone time as fertile ground for imagination, you can actually look forward to it. One moment you're quietly sipping tea by yourself, the next you've dreamed up a clever solution for a work project or a new direction for your personal goals. It's exciting!

Give yourself little assignments to cultivate creativity in solitude. For example, on your next solo walk, decide to mentally design your dream house or come up with an alternate ending to a movie you watched. There's no right or wrong – it's just play for your mind. If an idea grabs you, jot it down when you get home. Many authors, inventors, and creators keep journals precisely to catch those fleeting inspirations from quiet moments. Even if you don't consider yourself a "creative" person, you absolutely have the capacity for original thought. Solitude simply provides the *stage* for those thoughts to perform.

Research supports this: one article in *Harvard Business Review* found that people often experience their best insights not when straining for them, but when engaged in simple, unrelated activities in peace and quiet. In other words, you might solve that pesky problem while gardening alone or figure out lyrics for a song while taking a long bath. By intentionally giving yourself these quiet pockets of alone time, you're creating opportunities for inspiration to strike. And when it does, it feels almost magical – that delightful surprise of "Why didn't I think of this sooner?!"

To encourage your creative side, set up an inviting environment for your solo time. Maybe you have a cozy chair by a window that becomes your reading and sketching nook. Perhaps you light a scented candle or play soft instrumental music in the background as you paint or write. These little rituals signal your brain that it's safe to relax and let ideas flow. Over time, you'll start to cherish these solitude-fueled creative sessions. Instead of associating "alone" with boredom, you'll know that quiet breeds imagination – and you might even get excited for an evening by yourself because it's a chance to dream, invent, or refine your ideas.

And if you ever feel stuck or bored when alone, try leaning into that boredom rather than fighting it – psychologist Dr. Rita Watson suggests that even mild boredom can be a precursor to creativity, as it encourages daydreaming. So the next time you catch yourself with nothing to do on a quiet afternoon, resist the urge to immediately grab your phone. Instead, let your mind drift – who knows where it might lead? By trusting in these quiet moments and your own inner voice, you transform solitude into a wellspring of creativity and inspiration.

Self-Improvement and Goal Setting

Solitude isn't just a time for hobbies and daydreams – it's also the perfect opportunity for self-improvement. When you're not distracted by social demands or the buzz of notifications, you can focus fully on *your* aspirations. Think of your alone time as a personal training ground where you can build the life you want, step by step. Without anyone else around, it's easier to ask yourself honest questions: *What do I want to achieve? What skills do I want to develop? How can I become a better version of myself?* In quiet moments, you can hear the answers more clearly. In fact, solitude can be a powerful tool for self-discovery and goal-setting – it allows you to reflect on what truly matters to you.

Perhaps you have a fitness goal, like running a 5K or doing a certain number of yoga sessions. Being alone means you can create a workout schedule that suits you, without worrying about a buddy's availability or feeling self-conscious at the gym. Maybe you want to advance your career or academics – you could set aside solitary evenings to take online courses or read up on subjects in a focused way. When you're by yourself, you can deep dive into learning without interruptions. Solitude provides the concentration and space needed for deep work on yourself. Over time, those independent study hours or practice sessions add up to real progress.

Here are a few tips to effectively work on your goals during alone time (no accountability partner needed!):

1. **Write Down Your Plan:** Start by clarifying what you want to achieve. Journal about your goals or make a checklist. Writing a concrete plan gives you direction. For example, if your goal is to learn a new language, your plan could be "Practice Spanish on Duolingo for 20 minutes daily" or "Learn 10 new vocabulary

words each week." Putting it on paper makes it feel official and motivating.

2. **Break It Into Steps & Make a Routine:** Big goals can be daunting, so break them into bite-sized steps you can tackle solo. If you aim to get fit, the first step might be "Go for a 15-minute walk each morning." If you want to write a book, step one could be "Draft 500 words every weeknight." Establish a routine around your chosen activity – maybe you always do it in the morning before others wake up, or late at night when the house is quiet. Consistency is easier when you tie it to your alone time ritual.

3. **Track Your Progress:** Keep a log of what you've done. This could be a simple habit tracker, a diary entry, or an app where you check off each day you practiced. Tracking your progress not only keeps you accountable to *yourself*, but it also provides a confidence boost. You'll see proof that you're moving forward, which is especially important when you don't have someone else cheering you on daily. And yes, celebrate those check marks – each one represents time you invested in *you*!

4. **Celebrate Milestones (By Yourself):** When you hit a milestone on your own, take time to acknowledge it. Maybe you treat yourself to a nice solo movie night or a fancy dessert when you complete a month of consistent workouts or finish an online course. Don't dismiss your solo achievements just because no one else is around clapping – *be your own cheerleader.* You might

even share the news in a journal or tell a close friend later, but in the moment, allow yourself to feel genuinely proud. Each personal victory, no matter how small, is building your self-confidence.

As you follow these steps, you'll likely find that achieving goals on your own builds a special kind of inner confidence. Without needing an audience or outside validation, you learn to rely on yourself and recognize your capabilities. Indeed, spending time working on personal goals alone forces you to become self-reliant and resilient. One resource on thriving in solitude put it perfectly: *"Alone time builds self-reliance. Facing your thoughts and solving problems solo fosters confidence and prepares you for life's challenges.".* In other words, when you tackle a challenge by yourself – say, sticking to a budget for a month or finally decluttering your apartment solo – you prove to yourself that you can handle things independently. That confidence carries over into other areas of life, counteracting feelings of helplessness or loneliness.

Moreover, being alone allows you to focus intensely. Distraction-free solitude can sharpen your attention and productivity, making your efforts more effective. Think about students who prefer to study alone in a quiet library – they do it because it helps them absorb material better. In the same way, you might find you make more progress on a coding project or musical instrument during solo practice than you ever did in a busy group class. There are fewer interruptions, and you can work at your own optimal pace. Even research suggests that quality solo time can make you more productive. So if you have a personal goal requiring deep work, cherish those alone sessions as prime time to get into a "flow" state.

A great example is someone learning to play guitar alone. Without fear of judgment, you can hit wrong notes freely until you improve. You might dedicate 30 minutes each night to practicing chords. At first, progress could feel slow, but after a few weeks, you realize you can play a whole song. That accomplishment is *yours* – you earned it without anyone prodding you. That experience not only makes you a better guitarist; it also reminds you that you're capable of growth through your own discipline. Over time, these solo accomplishments pile up, and so does your mental strength. You'll start to approach new goals with less fear, because you trust your ability to stick with things, even alone.

Finally, remember to be patient and kind to yourself in this self-improvement journey. When you're alone, it can be easy to either slack off *or* to be too hard on yourself since no one's watching. Try to find a balance: hold yourself accountable, but also give yourself grace on the tough days. If you miss a planned study session or your workout didn't happen, don't spiral into loneliness or self-criticism. Use your solitude for positive self-talk: "Okay, I missed today, but I can continue tomorrow." Being a good companion to yourself means encouraging yourself the way a true friend would. Keep the tone of your alone time supportive and constructive. Over weeks and months, you'll likely see remarkable growth – you might lose that weight, gain that certificate, master that skill – and you'll know *you did it for you*. That sense of independence and competence is one of the best antidotes to feeling lonely. When you improve yourself in solitude, you realize you're never truly alone – you have *goals* and *dreams* keeping you company and a stronger version of you emerging from within.

Celebrating Independence – "Solo Adventures" and Achievements

There's a special thrill in doing something big all by yourself and realizing you not only survived, but thrived. This section is all about celebrating your independence through "solo adventures" – those bold acts that you might ordinarily wait to do with a friend or partner, but can actually be incredibly rewarding on your own. It's time to occasionally be your own hero and prove that fun and fulfillment don't require an entourage. By embracing such solo adventures, you reinforce the idea that *your happiness isn't contingent on others*, and you create memories that are yours and yours alone.

Perhaps there's a trip you've been fantasizing about – a picturesque coastal drive, a visit to a city overseas, or a spiritual retreat – but you've been postponing it, waiting for someone to join you. Maybe every time you bring it up, friends bail or schedules never align. What if you took the plunge and went by yourself? It sounds intimidating, but countless people cite solo travel as a life-changing, liberating experience. As one psychologist and avid traveler explains, taking a trip alone lets you access a richer array of thoughts and sensations, because you're not distracted by another person's agenda. You can be entirely *present* in your new surroundings. You decide where to go, what to eat, when to wake up – total freedom. Initially it might feel strange to navigate a new place solo, but that challenge is exactly what builds your confidence. "When traveling alone, you can be anyone you please," and you give yourself permission to try new ways of being, notes psychologist Francine Toder.

Take it from those who've done it: one seasoned solo traveler named Laura shared that *"traveling halfway around the world alone is liberating, empowering. Making friends in new places is priceless."* She found that any loneliness was outweighed by the freedom and personal growth she experienced on her journey. Similarly, many women and men report that doing things like dining out or attending events alone, which once scared them, turned out to be empowering milestones. It's like proving to yourself, "I am enough. I can enjoy this on my own." In the words of a 24-year-old named Samantha who started going to concerts, museums, and hikes by herself, *"It's like I have this little secret with myself—this experience that was just for me. Nobody knows it was a really lovely, profound time.".* That sentiment beautifully captures the quiet pride of a solo adventure – it becomes a special memory between you and yourself.

Now, a solo adventure doesn't have to be an international voyage (though if you feel up for it, go for it!). It could be as simple as treating yourself to a fancy dinner at that restaurant you've always wanted to try, or going to a concert of your favorite band without a plus-one. The first time you do this, you might feel a bit self-conscious – "Will people notice I'm alone?" – but trust me, most people are too busy with their own lives to care. And those who do notice might even admire your independence. A therapist who often coaches people through this recommends reframing the experience: you're not "alone" – you're on a date with yourself. Walk in with confidence, order exactly what *you* want, and savor it. You might end up chatting with friendly strangers or simply enjoying your own company. Either way, you'll realize that an evening out solo can be just as enjoyable as one spent with others – sometimes even more so, because you have complete latitude to do what pleases you.

If larger outings feel daunting, start small and build up. Maybe begin with a low-stakes outing like a movie matinee or a coffee at a cute café by yourself. These simpler solo experiences will show you that being out and about alone is genuinely no big deal – it can even be fun. One expert suggests ranking activities from least to most intimidating and starting at the easy end. For example, grabbing coffee alone might be a 2 out of 10 on your fear scale, whereas a weekend road trip alone is a 9. Do the coffee a few times, then try a meal out, then perhaps a day trip, and so on. Each positive experience will "grow your capacity to take on other challenges". You're basically training your brain to be comfortable flying solo.

When you do venture into bigger solo adventures – say you finally book that trip to the mountains or attend a music festival on your own – take time to celebrate your courage and independence. These are not small feats! Many people never dare to do these things alone, so recognize what a rockstar you are for doing it. Journal about what you saw and felt. Take photos not just to show others, but as mementos for yourself ("I did this!"). A helpful habit is, after each solo adventure, to reflect on what you learned and enjoyed. Maybe you discovered you actually love the tranquility of a long train ride with just your thoughts. Or you navigated a foreign city by map and felt a surge of confidence. Perhaps you had a meaningful encounter with someone new precisely because you were solo and more open to conversation. These wins deserve to be acknowledged. Give yourself credit – perhaps even literally give yourself a *certificate of achievement* in your mind for "Solo Trip Completed" or "Museum Visit Mastered." It might sound cheesy, but internal validation is powerful.

Importantly, through these experiences you'll likely find that accomplishments don't need an audience to be fulfilling. Sure, it's nice to have someone clap for you, but accomplishing something on your own – and knowing in your heart that you did it – can be just as rewarding. It builds a quiet self-assurance. You no longer wait for life to happen to you or for others to join in – you make your own plans and carry them out. As a popular saying goes, *a bit of "flying solo" might be exactly what you need.* If you've been waiting endlessly for friends to do that hiking trip or go to that art exhibit, consider this a sign to go anyway. You might end up having a wonderful time and wondering why you didn't try it sooner.

Finally, every solo adventure, big or small, reinforces that you are capable of enjoying life on your own terms. You start to realize that being alone is *not* equivalent to being lonely – it can be a form of self-care and empowerment. One therapist notes that spending time doing things alone pushes you out of your comfort zone, and *"that grows your capacity to take on other challenges in your day-to-day life."* In other words, today's solo museum day could make you braver to tackle tomorrow's job interview or life decision without hand-holding. You're training the muscle of independence. And the best part? You're also making priceless memories. When you think back on that beautiful sunset you watched from the hill you hiked up alone, or the concert where you danced like no one was watching (because no one who knew you *was* watching!), you'll feel a swell of happiness. Those moments belong solely to you – a testament to your self-sufficiency and courage.

As you grow more comfortable doing things solo, you'll likely start to feel an unexpected sense of companionship…with *yourself.* You've proven to be pretty great company after all. You can laugh to yourself at an observation, move at your own pace, and follow your whims without compromise. This realization – that you can truly enjoy your own company – is perhaps the ultimate prize of thriving in solitude. At that point, being alone is no longer something to dread; it's something to occasionally cherish. You're not lonely – you're just independently content. And that is a strength that will serve you for a lifetime.

Growing and thriving in solitude is all about mindset. When you approach alone time as an opportunity for passion projects, creativity, self-improvement, and bold solo adventures, it transforms into something positive and nourishing. You start to see solitude not as emptiness, but as space – space for your interests, your ideas, and your personal growth. You learn that your worth isn't defined by the presence of others, but by how you choose to spend the time with *yourself.* By finding purpose in hobbies, sparking inspiration in quiet moments, achieving goals on your own, and celebrating independent adventures, you build a life where being alone doesn't feel lonely. It feels empowering. You've cultivated a strong, fulfilled person within – someone who knows that, in the end, *you are never truly alone when you like the person you're alone with*. So go ahead: embrace your solitude, and watch yourself grow and thrive. Your journey to enjoying your own company is one of the greatest adventures you'll ever have.

Chapter 6
Surviving Rejection – Staying Strong and Resilient Through Setbacks

R ejection hurts. There's no way around it – whether it's the sting of an unrequited crush, the disappointment of not landing a job, or the ache of feeling excluded by friends. It's something every single one of us goes through sooner or later. Yet when it happens, it *feels* deeply personal and isolating. In this chapter, we'll explore why rejection affects us so profoundly and, more importantly, how to cope with it in healthy ways. You'll learn how to keep rejection in perspective, take care of your emotional wounds, and come out of setbacks stronger than before. Rejection is painful, but it does not have to diminish your self-worth or keep you from living a fulfilling life. Let's dive into why it hurts so much and how to stay resilient through it all.

Why Rejection Hurts (and Happens to Everyone)

Rejection is a universal experience. No matter who you are or what path you're on, you will face rejection at some point. It might be a romantic partner ending a relationship, an employer choosing another candidate, or friends moving on without you. Knowing this doesn't make the pain magically disappear, but it does help to remember you're not alone. Everyone – even the most successful, charismatic people – has felt the sting of not being chosen or wanted. In fact, one psychologist emphasizes that rejection is *inevitable* in life, and our goal shouldn't be to avoid it completely (since we can't), but to handle it in the healthiest way possible. So if you're feeling hurt by a recent setback, remind yourself that *millions of others have felt exactly like you do*. There's nothing strange or "weak" about feeling pain when rejected – it's a sign that you're human, with normal human needs for acceptance.

Biologically, we're wired to seek acceptance. Humans are inherently social creatures. For our distant ancestors, being rejected by the tribe wasn't just sad – it was dangerous. Losing social connections could threaten one's survival. As a result, our brains evolved to treat social rejection as a serious threat. Modern brain research shows that an experience of rejection activates the same areas of the brain as physical pain does. In other words, a heartbreak or snub can *hurt like a real injury* because, neurologically, your brain registers it similarly to being physically hurt. No wonder it stings so badly! The *dorsal anterior cingulate cortex* and *anterior insula* – regions that process the "ouch" of physical pain – also light up when you feel socially rejected. This overlap is why a harsh rejection can literally feel like a punch in the gut. On an evolutionary level, this pain is actually an alarm system. It developed to alert us that our social bonds (which historically meant safety and support) are in danger. In prehistoric times, a person who didn't care about being cast out might not survive long. So, if you feel heartbroken or devastated by rejection, remember: your reaction is completely normal. Your brain is responding exactly as it was designed to, and *anyone* in your situation would feel a similar wound.

Emotionally, rejection strikes at our self-worth. Beyond the biology, rejection often triggers a flood of negative emotions and thoughts. You might start wondering *"What's wrong with me?"* or *"Why wasn't I good enough?"*. It can feel like a personal verdict on your value. Psychologically, when someone we care about (or an opportunity we invested in) turns us down, it's common to internalize it as a reflection of our worth. You might feel ashamed, inadequate, or not valued, especially if the rejection came out of the blue. For example, being unexpectedly broken up with can leave you questioning your attractiveness or lovability. Not getting a job you hoped for might make you doubt your skills. These reactions are intense but very typical. The hurt can even dredge up old insecurities from past rejections, compounding the pain. One clinical psychologist notes that new rejection can revive *"evidence"* you've collected of not being lovable or worthy, leading you to build a case against yourself in your own mind. It's like each rejection echoes earlier ones, reinforcing that sting. But as convincing as those feelings are, it's crucial to realize they are *emotional reactions*, not objective truth about you.

Rejection doesn't mean you lack value. This point is so important that we'll say it again: being rejected is not a judgment of your inherent worth. It may feel that way – when someone you love leaves, or when you're passed over for an opportunity, it's easy to conclude *"I'm not good enough"*. In reality, rejection often has more to do with the other person's preferences or the circumstances than with any failing on your part. A job rejection, for instance, might simply mean the company had a candidate who better fit their specific needs – not that you were unqualified. A romantic rejection could mean the other person isn't ready for a relationship or is looking for a different type of partner – not that you are unlovable. We all tend to be a bit *self-centric* in interpreting rejection (after all, we experience it as happening *to us*), but often the reasons are outside our control. Timing, context, or the other party's situation play huge roles. Everyone faces rejection sooner or later, and often it says nothing about who you are as a person. Reminding yourself of this perspective can ease the personal sting. Think of it this way: someone else's decision or opinion – an employer's choice, a romantic interest's feelings – does not determine your value. Your worth comes from within, from your own qualities, values, and how you treat others, not from external validation. It can be liberating to realize that *one setback or one person's "no" can't take away your intrinsic value*. You're still the same capable, worthy individual you were before the rejection. Keeping this truth in mind is the first step toward not letting rejection crush your self-esteem.

Not Taking Rejection Personally

When rejection happens, it's easy to take it as a personal attack or a sign that *"there's something wrong with me."* Our minds are incredibly quick to create a narrative around the experience. Often, that story is harsh and self-blaming: *"I'm not good enough," "I'll always be alone," "I must have messed everything up."* These thoughts may rush in automatically, but it's crucial to recognize them for what they are – distortions, not facts. In this section, we'll look at how to catch those inaccurate thoughts and respond to rejection without turning it into a personal indictment.

Beware of the false stories you tell yourself. After a painful rejection, many people start catastrophizing or generalizing. For example, if someone you were dating ends things, you might think, *"I'll never find love – I'm going to die alone."* If you don't get a job offer, you might conclude, *"No one will ever hire me; I'm just not cut out for this."* These extreme conclusions are understandable in the heat of emotion, but they are not truthful predictions of your future. They're reflections of how hurt and disappointed you feel in the moment. Psychologists note that when we're rejected, we tend to zero in on supposed personal flaws and forget about all the external factors at play. Emotions like sadness or shame act like a distortion lens, making us interpret the situation in the most negative (and self-critical) way. One therapist explains that our brains often overlook non-personal factors and automatically assume the rejection was due to our shortcomings. In reality, that assumption is usually way off base.

Consider this common scenario: You muster the courage to submit a creative project or a proposal at work, and it gets turned down. In the aftermath, your mind might start listing every reason you weren't up to par – "Maybe I'm just bad at this, maybe I'm not talented enough, I shouldn't have tried." But maybe the truth is simply that the company's budget was tight, or they decided to go in a different direction this time. In fact, one writer shares that her story pitches get rejected all the time, but instead of assuming her ideas are "crap," she reminds herself that editors might have recently covered that topic or had no budget, or that she could tweak the idea and try again. By considering these *alternative explanations*, she prevents herself from spiraling into self-doubt. The goal, as she and her psychologist colleagues suggest, is to fact-check the story you're telling yourself about the rejection. Step back and ask: *"Is it really me that was the problem here? Or could something else explain this?"* Nine times out of ten, you'll find plenty of impersonal reasons. Maybe the timing wasn't right. Maybe the other person had their own issues or commitments. Maybe the fit just wasn't there – and that's nobody's fault.

Challenge the "not good enough" narrative. A powerful strategy to not take rejection personally is to actively question those negative conclusions your mind jumps to. Psychologist Molly Burrets advises taking a rational, objective look at the situation to *"let go of an unhealthy and inaccurate narrative that you're not good enough or will never be good enough."*. What does that mean in practice? It means that when you catch yourself thinking, *"I wasn't chosen because I'm defective in some way,"* you pause and dispute that thought. Ask yourself: *"What evidence do I have for that belief? Is it really true, or am I just hurt right now?"* Often, you'll realize the evidence is either flimsy or nonexistent. For example, being rejected after a few dates might simply mean you and the other person weren't a match – not that you're unattractive or unworthy. Or not getting a call back from a job might mean the company hired an internal candidate. Telling yourself *"I'm just not good at anything"* is not only untrue, it's also unfair to yourself. As one expert points out, you can usually identify aspects of a rejection that truly had nothing to do with your personal shortcomings. Recognize those and you'll see that the rejection wasn't a clear judgment on you as a whole.

One helpful exercise is to reframe the rejection from a different angle. Try to look at it as an outsider or from the other person's point of view.

A psychologist, Dr. Lauren Phillips, suggests considering what might be going on with the person or institution that rejected you. Maybe that hiring manager had dozens of highly qualified candidates and could only choose one. Maybe the person who declined a second date had just come out of a tough breakup and isn't ready for a new relationship. When you imagine reasons like these, you begin to see the rejection "wasn't about me personally." In fact, Dr. Phillips explains that doing this can make you feel calmer and break out of the *"them vs. me"* mindset of feeling singled out. By understanding that the other party has their own context, you can soften the blow to your self-esteem. It becomes easier to think, *"Okay, they had their reasons; this isn't just a condemnation of me."*

Replace self-blame with self-compassion. Often after rejection, our inner voice can be downright cruel. We blame ourselves, listing every supposed flaw. But beating yourself up will only deepen the wounds. Instead, make a conscious effort to talk to yourself the way you'd talk to a dear friend who just got rejected. Would you ever tell a friend "Yeah, you got rejected because you're not good enough and you'll be alone forever"? Of course not! You'd probably say something supportive like, *"This opportunity just wasn't the right fit – something better will come,"* or *"Their loss! You're a wonderful person and I know this doesn't define you."* You deserve the same kindness from yourself. In fact, one expert in abandonment recovery suggests an exercise: imagine the hurt, rejected part of you is like a small, wounded child who needs love and comfort. How would you treat that child? You'd be gentle, understanding, and reassuring. Try to extend that gentleness to yourself. Remind yourself of your strengths and positive qualities, even if you don't feel very confident right now. It might help to literally list them out: "I am a caring friend," "I'm good at my job," "I have overcome tough stuff before." By affirming what you do well and what makes you *you*, you push back against the narrative that one rejection defines you.

Keep in mind that one person's opinion or one missed chance doesn't determine your future. It's so easy to give a rejection the power to dictate how we see ourselves. But no single event has that kind of power unless we allow it. As the old saying goes, "Don't let a bad day make you think you have a bad life." Similarly, don't let one rejection trick you into believing you have a bad self. You are more than this moment. Remind yourself that *you have inherent worth that isn't up for debate.* Sometimes you might have to actively say to yourself, "I'm still worthy and lovable, no matter what *they* think." It's not about ego, it's about balance – not letting a negative experience overshadow all the positives of who you are.

Practical strategies to not internalize rejection: It can be helpful to have a few go-to tactics when you catch yourself taking a rejection too personally. Here are some ideas:

- **Journal or write it out:** Putting your feelings on paper can slow down a racing mind and bring some clarity. Write down exactly what you're thinking and feeling about the rejection. You might even write the story you're telling yourself (e.g., "I didn't get the job because I'm incompetent"). Seeing it written can help you start to question it. In fact, research shows journaling can counteract negative thought spirals and help you view your experience more objectively. After venting on the page, you might notice an *"unhelpful narrative"* lurking – that's your chance to correct it.

- **Fact-check and reframe:** As discussed, challenge the assumptions in your narrative. If you wrote "I'll never succeed," ask "Is that really true? What evidence is there to the contrary?" Force yourself to list at least one or two alternative explanations for what happened (e.g., "Maybe they had budget constraints," or "Maybe he isn't ready for commitment"). The act of considering other angles helps break the spell of *self-blame*. It reminds you that reality is more complex than "I'm just not good enough." Experts say this kind of rational re-framing can "remind you that you aren't totally at fault" and help you let go of the inaccurate notion that you're permanently not enough.

- **Consider their perspective:** Put yourself in the other person's shoes just for a moment. This isn't to diminish your own feelings, but to see that the rejection likely wasn't a personal crusade against you. If a friend suddenly cancels plans or drifts away, could it be that they're overwhelmed in their own life? If an interviewer chose someone else, could it be that candidate had more direct experience rather than you lacking something? When you *humanize* the other side, the rejection feels less like an attack. It can even foster a bit of empathy – for instance, you might realize *"hey, they've got their own struggles, it wasn't about hurting me."* This perspective can be surprisingly freeing.

- **Remind yourself of your worth:** After a hit to your ego, deliberately do things that reinforce a positive sense of self. This might mean spending time with people who appreciate you, or engaging in an activity you excel at. One psychologist calls this "connecting with things (or people) that make you feel good about yourself". If you love painting, paint something. If you're a great cook, make a meal. Go play that sport you're good at or re-read a kind message someone sent you. These experiences validate the fact that you *are* skilled, likable, and talented – whatever negative thoughts rejection conjured were *not the whole truth*. Surround yourself, even temporarily, with reminders of what makes you awesome. As Dr. Burrets puts it, seek out situations that let you shine and people who make you feel valued, and have a "boundary" against those that make you question your worth in this vulnerable time. A night laughing with your best friends or achieving a small win in a hobby can reinforce that *you're still you*, and nobody's rejection can take away your strengths.

By consciously *not* taking rejection as a personal failing, you protect your self-esteem. This doesn't mean you ignore any lessons (we'll talk about learning from setbacks later), but it means you refuse to let your inner critic run wild. You are allowed to feel hurt – of course you will, you're human. But you don't have to add suffering on top of pain by tearing yourself down. As the saying goes, pain is inevitable, but suffering is optional. By controlling your interpretation and self-talk, you can experience the pain of rejection without it metastasizing into long-term damage to your identity.

Healing Through Self-Care and Support

Think of an emotional rejection as you would a physical wound. If you cut your hand, you'd clean it, put a bandage on, and give it time to heal – you wouldn't poke at it constantly or pour salt in it. Yet when it comes to emotional wounds, like the pain of rejection, we often do the opposite: we *ruminate* (the mental equivalent of poking a wound) or even punish ourselves further with harsh self-talk. To heal from rejection, you need to practice emotional first aid – tending kindly to the wound so it can mend. This section offers practical steps for recovering emotionally after a rejection. By using self-care and leaning on support, you can soothe the pain and rebuild your strength.

Give yourself permission to hurt (temporarily). The first step in healing is acknowledging that you're hurt. It's normal to feel upset, sad, or angry after a rejection. Suppressing those emotions or pretending "I'm fine" when you're not can actually prolong your pain. Instead, allow yourself a period to grieve the lost opportunity or relationship. This might mean having a good cry, writing in a journal about how you feel, or just spending a quiet evening processing your thoughts. As one guide advises, *"It's normal to feel upset... Don't try to suppress your emotions or pretend it doesn't hurt. Acknowledge the pain, process your feelings, and give yourself time and space to heal.".* You might find it helpful to engage in rituals that let the feelings out – listen to music that matches your mood, watch a movie that makes you cry, talk it out with someone you trust. This is the emotional equivalent of cleaning a wound: it might sting at first, but it ensures proper healing rather than infection. Important: set a gentle boundary for yourself so that this feeling phase doesn't become indefinite wallowing. It's healthy to be sad for a while; it's unhealthy to decide "I will be miserable forever." Trust that the intensity of the pain will lessen with time, especially if you care for yourself along the way.

Replace self-criticism with self-compassion. We touched on this in the previous section, but in the healing phase it's absolutely crucial. Treat yourself with the same care and kindness you'd offer to a loved one who was hurt. This might involve a deliberate self-care routine: maybe you take a long warm bath to relax, or go for calming walks in nature, or indulge in a favorite comfort food without guilt. When you notice self-critical thoughts (like "How could I have been so stupid?" or "I'm such a loser for getting this upset"), consciously counter them with a compassionate perspective: "I'm hurting right now, and that's okay. I did my best, and I deserve care while I heal." Some people find it helpful to literally give themselves a hug or speak out loud words of comfort. It might feel awkward, but it powerfully signals to your brain that *you are safe and loved*, even if one situation didn't work out. Mental health experts often suggest visualization techniques: for example, picture yourself as a small, wounded child and imagine giving that child a warm hug and reassurance. This can awaken your nurturing side toward yourself. Research on self-compassion has found that being kind to yourself can buffer the negative effects of rejection and speed emotional recovery. So, next time you catch your inner voice saying something mean, pause and rephrase it into something caring. Over time, these small acts of self-kindness add up, helping you regain confidence and peace.

Take care of your basic needs. It sounds overly simple, but in the aftermath of rejection, basic self-care is *paramount*. Stress and emotional pain can take a toll on the body, so it's important to support yourself with adequate sleep, nutrition, and physical activity. Try to maintain a consistent sleep schedule – being well-rested will make you more emotionally resilient. Eat foods that give you genuine energy and nourishment (while it's fine to enjoy some ice cream or comfort food, don't fall into a pattern of skipping meals or subsisting on junk because you feel down). Movement can also be a great healer: even if you just go out for a short walk, physical activity releases endorphins that can improve your mood and help clear your mind. Think of exercise as a way of empowering yourself rather than a chore. A jog, a yoga session, or dancing around your living room can remind you that your body is alive and strong, which can translate into mental strength as well. These self-care basics are akin to keeping a wound clean and protected – they create an environment where healing can happen. When you take the time to care for your body, you're also sending a message to yourself that *you matter*. You're worth the effort, and you deserve to feel better.

Seek support – you don't have to go it alone. Just because you're learning to be comfortable alone doesn't mean you should *isolate* when you're hurting. In fact, one of the best remedies for the pain of rejection is to reach out to people who care about you. Rejection tends to make us feel *disconnected*, destabilizing our fundamental need to belong. Counteract that by connecting with your support network. Call your most understanding friend and vent about what happened. Meet up with a family member who always has your back. If you feel you don't have anyone to turn to, consider joining a support group or even online communities where people share similar experiences – sometimes just hearing "I've been through that too" from someone else can be incredibly validating. Research has shown that reconnecting with those who value and accept you soothes the emotional pain after a rejection. Simply being around people who appreciate you will reinforce that one rejection is not the whole world. Maybe you didn't get that job, but your friends still love your sense of humor. Maybe a romantic partner left, but your sibling still thinks the world of you. Let your supporters remind you of your worth. As a guide on rejection recovery notes, "rally whatever social support is available… Seek out company and connection to refill your sense of belonging". If you're someone who tends to withdraw when upset, challenge yourself to reach out *even just a little*. Send a text to a friend or say yes to a casual get-together. You might be surprised how much better it feels to share a laugh or even some tears with someone, instead of stewing in solitude.

At times, support might also mean professional help. If a particular rejection has hit you extremely hard – for example, triggering a depressive episode or old trauma – talking to a therapist can be enormously helpful. There's no shame in seeking counseling; a trained therapist can provide a safe space to process your feelings and teach you coping skills tailored to your situation. They can also help you challenge any deeply ingrained negative beliefs that rejection has brought up. Think of therapy as a more intensive form of self-care, like seeing a doctor for a serious wound. Sometimes, the emotional injury from rejection (especially repeated or severe rejection) can cut deep. A therapist is like a skilled surgeon for those emotional wounds, helping ensure they heal cleanly without festering into something worse.

Engage in activities that bring you joy or peace. While you don't want to use distractions to avoid ever facing your feelings, it's perfectly healthy – even important – to continue doing things that make you happy. Rejection can occupy your mind like a dark cloud; positive activities provide rays of sunlight that break through. What brings you even small glimmers of joy? Maybe it's watching your favorite comedy show, or baking bread, or playing video games, or doing arts and crafts. Giving yourself permission to enjoy something during a tough time is not "ignoring reality" – it's a form of resilience. It's saying, "This hurtful thing happened, but I still deserve moments of laughter and comfort." In fact, those moments help *heal* by reducing stress and reminding you that life still has pleasant experiences to offer. If it's hard to motivate yourself, invite a friend to join you (say, go on a hike together or have a movie night). Their presence can help you engage with the activity rather than staying lost in your head.

Another healing activity to consider is creative expression. Writing a poem or song about how you feel, painting or drawing, or playing music can all be cathartic. You're essentially channeling that pain into art, which can both process the emotion and create something beautiful out of it. Many great works of art, music, and literature have been born from the creators' experiences of rejection and heartache. Your goal doesn't have to be to create a masterpiece; it's about expressing yourself and releasing the pent-up feelings in a constructive way.

Lastly, remember to be patient with yourself. Just as a physical wound might take days or weeks to fully heal, emotional wounds also need time. There might be days you feel like you've turned the corner, only to unexpectedly feel a twinge of hurt again. Healing is not perfectly linear. But if you consistently practice self-care and reach out for support, you *will* notice the pain easing over time. One day, you'll realize the rejection is just a memory and it no longer hurts like it used to. By treating yourself with compassion and surrounding yourself with kindness, you're not only healing – you're also building up emotional strength for the future.

Bouncing Back Stronger – Lessons from Rejection

Here's the silver lining about rejection: as painful as it is, it can *ultimately make you stronger*. Think of rejection as a teacher or a forge – it can impart lessons and forge resilience that success alone might not have given you. Many people look back on a rejection that once felt devastating and realize it was a turning point that led them to grow, improve, or find a better path. In this section, we'll explore how to bounce back from setbacks not just intact, but improved. We'll see how rejections can carry valuable lessons, how surviving them boosts your confidence, and how some of the world's most successful individuals turned rejection into fuel for greatness.

Every setback carries a lesson. When you're in the immediate aftermath of a rejection, it's hard to see anything beyond the hurt. But once the initial sting subsides, it can be incredibly useful to reflect on *"What can I learn from this?"*. This isn't about blaming yourself or obsessing over the past – it's about gently mining the experience for wisdom that might help you in the future. Sometimes, a rejection reveals an area for growth or a misalignment in your life that you hadn't recognized. For example, not getting a job might motivate you to strengthen certain skills or realize that another field is actually where you belong. A failed relationship might teach you more about what you truly need in a partner or highlight patterns you want to change. One individual shared that after many painful rejections in both love and career, she had a lightbulb moment: these things were happening for a reason, nudging her to reassess her path. She began to see rejection as an opportunity to become more acquainted with different parts of herself and to make changes where needed. Instead of viewing each rejection as merely a loss, she asked *"Why might this have happened, and what could I do differently?"* Not in a self-critical way, but in a curious, growth-oriented way. By doing so, she found that *every job she was denied opened the door to new, better opportunities, and every heartbreak led her closer to the right relationship.* Her perspective shifted from seeing rejection as the end of something to seeing it as a redirection towards something else.

You can use a similar approach. After you've healed a bit, take some time to reflect: Was there anything this rejection taught me about what I truly want or don't want? Did it reveal a strength I didn't know I had (like courage – hey, you put yourself out there!) or a skill I could develop more? Maybe it simply taught you that you can survive something you thought you couldn't. Often the lesson is as simple as understanding yourself better. Surviving a romantic rejection, for instance, might teach you that you actually value your independence more than you realized, or that you want to communicate your needs more clearly next time. A professional rejection might teach you to be more prepared, or it might free you to pursue a different role that suits you better. Sometimes, rejection forces a course correction: it points you away from one path and, in doing so, guides you to another. The key is to approach this reflection with a gentle, constructive mindset. Ask not "What's wrong with me?" but "What can I take away from this experience that will help me in the future?". By framing it as a learning experience, you transform rejection from a purely painful event into a stepping stone for personal development.

Resilience: the hidden gift of rejection. Resilience is the ability to withstand adversity and bounce back from difficulties. Like a muscle, it often grows strongest when it's been tested. Each time you go through a rejection and come out on the other side, you're building that resilience. You're proving to yourself, *"I can handle this. It hurts, but it didn't break me."* In fact, living through rejection can increase your confidence to take future risks. Why? Because once you've experienced the worst-case scenario (not getting the job, being told "no," etc.) and you see that you *survived*, it becomes a little less scary to put yourself out there again. You might think, *"Well, the last time I asked someone out I was turned down, but hey, I lived. I was able to move on. So if it happens again, I know I'll be okay."* This mindset is incredibly freeing. It doesn't mean you *want* to be rejected again, but the fear of it holds less power over you.

Some therapists even encourage people to intentionally collect a few rejections – not because rejection is fun (it's not), but to demystify it and reduce the paralyzing fear around it. There's a concept called "rejection therapy" where you purposefully make harmless requests that are likely to be refused (like asking for a free coffee refill) just to practice tolerating rejection and realize it's not the end of the world. It's a bit unconventional, but it underscores the idea that experiencing rejection and realizing *"I'm still okay"* builds resilience and courage. One author in a TED Talk described rejection as a form of psychological exercise that, over time, strengthened him against the fear. He began even seeking out chances to be rejected, and found that as his fear went down, his success in other areas went up – because he was trying more, risking more, and thus getting more opportunities (and yes, some yeses too).

Even without formal "rejection therapy," simply living life and not shying away from opportunities will naturally bring a mix of rejections and acceptances. Each rejection can make you tougher. Think of it like tempering steel: you might go through the fire, but you emerge harder to break. After overcoming a painful setback, you might notice a new sense of confidence. You might tell yourself, "If I got through *that*, I can get through anything." This is not just empty positivity – it's a real, earned belief from experience. Surviving rejection proves your own resilience to yourself.

Real-world success stories: fuel from rejection. History and pop culture are full of examples of people who faced repeated rejection and used it as fuel to eventually achieve great success. Whenever you feel disheartened, it can help to remember these stories – they show that rejection is not a dead-end, just a detour. For instance, author Stephen King, one of the best-selling novelists of all time, had his first novel *Carrie* rejected 30 times by publishers. At one point, he was so frustrated he threw the manuscript in the trash! (His wife fished it out and told him to keep trying). King famously kept a nail on his wall to collect rejection letters; it eventually overflowed and he had to replace it with a bigger spike. Instead of giving up, he persisted – and when *Carrie* was finally published, it sold over a million copies in its first year and launched his legendary career. Imagine if he had taken those 30 rejections to mean "I'm not good enough to be a writer" – the world would have lost out on so many stories.

Another inspiring example is J.K. Rowling, the author of *Harry Potter*. Rowling was rejected by about a dozen publishers when trying to get her first Harry Potter book published. One publisher even told her not to quit her day job because children's books just don't make money. She was an unemployed single mother at the time, facing a lot of personal hardships. Many people would have given up, but she believed in her story. Finally, a small publishing house took a chance on her (encouraged by the chairman's young daughter who loved the first chapter). Today, J.K. Rowling is one of the best-selling authors in history and an inspiration to millions. Her series didn't just succeed; it became a global phenomenon. Those early rejections were *redirections* that led her to the right publisher and taught her perseverance.

These aren't isolated cases. *Gone with the Wind* by Margaret Mitchell was rejected 38 times before publication. Walt Disney was told he lacked creativity early in his career. Musician Elvis Presley was once fired after a performance and told, "You ain't goin' nowhere, son." The list goes on. In each case, the individual took the rejection not as a final verdict, but as motivation to keep improving or to prove the naysayers wrong. A modern editing company blog put it nicely: "Rejection refines us. Those who persist past it are survivors.". The people who ultimately succeed are often not the ones who never got rejected – they are the ones who *didn't quit* in spite of it.

Rejection as redirection. There's a popular saying: *"Rejection is just redirection."* Often, when you look back on a rejection, you can see how it sent you toward something better. Maybe that job you didn't get would have made you miserable, and the next one was a perfect fit. Maybe being rejected by one person freed you to meet someone who truly appreciates you. At the time, you might not see any "reason" for the setback – it just hurts. But hindsight often reveals a purpose. One writer reflected on her life and said, "Every time I thought I was being rejected from something good, I was actually being redirected to something better.". In her case, every job rejection led her to a new opportunity, every failed relationship guided her to personal growth and eventually to a happy marriage. While we don't have to believe that *every* rejection is fate or destiny, we can choose to give it a positive meaning. You can choose to tell yourself, *"This closed door is nudging me to find an open door elsewhere."*

Indeed, psychological research supports the idea that sometimes not getting what we want can lead us to what we *need*. The SELF magazine writer we discussed earlier shared that in retrospect, her painful rejections were actually course corrections. The college relationship that ended heartbreakingly made space for her to later meet her husband. The coveted start-up job she lost out on pushed her to focus on writing, which turned out to be a much more fulfilling career for her. As her therapist wisely told her, *"maybe not getting that thing points the arrow in a different direction."*. And that new direction can be full of wonderful surprises.

Next time you face rejection, it might help (after the initial pain subsides) to ask: *"What could this be redirecting me towards?"* It encourages hope and forward-thinking. Even if you don't have the answer yet, trusting that there *is* something better up ahead can keep you motivated to move on rather than give up. At the very least, seeing rejection this way can make you a bit less afraid of it. If you know that, in time, you can make something good out of even the worst setbacks, then rejection loses a lot of its terror. It becomes not a stop sign, but a signpost pointing you in a new direction.

Becoming stronger and wiser. Ultimately, handling rejection constructively will shape you into a stronger, wiser version of yourself. Each time you bounce back, you're a little more unshakable. You develop empathy (because having felt pain, you might become kinder to others who are hurting). You develop courage (because you know you can survive pain, you take bold chances). You also gain wisdom about life's ebbs and flows. People who've been through rejection often have a grounded perspective: they know that bad times don't last forever, and neither do good times – life is a series of cycles, and we can navigate them without losing ourselves.

By processing your rejections in a healthy way – feeling the pain, but refusing to let it define you or stop you – you build a form of emotional callus. Not a numbness, but a resilience. The goal isn't to never feel hurt again (we will always feel *something* when rejected, and that's okay), but to trust in your ability to recover and thrive regardless. When you truly internalize that, you become practically fearless. You won't be controlled by fear of hearing "no," because you'll know that even a "no" can lead to growth or a better "yes" elsewhere.

In fact, some of the most confident, self-assured people are those who've survived a lot of setbacks. They carry themselves with a quiet assurance, a knowledge that *"I can handle whatever comes."* That kind of confidence is unshakeable because it's built on real experience – you earned it by walking through the fire and coming out intact. And ironically, when you fear rejection less, you tend to attract more acceptance. People respond to that confidence and resilience; opportunities present themselves to those who keep putting themselves out there.

As we wrap up this chapter, remember this: rejection is not a dead end, it's a detour. It can hurt a lot, but it will not hurt forever. By not taking it personally, caring for yourself, and looking for the growth in the experience, you can turn what feels like a setback into a *setup* for your next success. The pain of rejection has lessons to teach and strength to give. Embrace those lessons, allow that strength to form, and carry on. You'll find that with each rejection you survive, you feel a little more comfortable in your own company and a lot less afraid of what the world might throw at you. In learning how to be alone without feeling lonely, knowing how to handle rejection is a pivotal skill – it ensures that even when others let you down, you won't let yourself down. You'll pick yourself up, value yourself even more, and step forward into whatever comes next, confident that you can not only survive, but thrive.

In the next chapter, we will continue building on this resilience and explore how to deepen the relationship with yourself, so that external setbacks like rejection shake you less and less. For now, give yourself a pat on the back for making it through the hard parts – every rejection you endure is proof of your courage. Keep that in mind, and you'll never truly be alone or defeated. You have *you*, and you are enough.

Chapter 7
Thriving in Your Own Company – A Fulfilling Life Ahead

Independence as Empowerment

Think back to when you first began this journey – being alone might have felt intimidating or even sad. Now, here you are at the final chapter, having transformed solitude from something scary into something empowering. You've learned to enjoy your own company and discovered that independence can be a tremendous source of freedom. When you're content alone, you no longer feel like life is on hold waiting for someone else's approval or presence. Instead, you can chart your own course and pursue your dreams on your own terms, with confidence and clarity.

True independence means knowing in your heart that you have the strength to handle challenges solo. Recall the earlier moments when you faced rejection or disappointment: rather than breaking you, those experiences taught you resilience. Standing on your own two feet, you realized you could survive setbacks without losing your sense of self-worth. Each time you navigated a challenge alone, you proved to yourself how capable you are. This self-reliance is incredibly empowering – it's like a quiet inner voice reminding you, "I've got this." Psychologists note that spending time alone can actually nurture this inner strength, helping to *"define and nurture our character"* and even *"grow our resilience and independence"*. In other words, your solo hours have been quietly hardening your armor and sharpening your identity.

Importantly, embracing independence doesn't mean shutting everyone out. This newfound strength isn't a rejection of others – it's simply a solid assurance that you can stand strong on your own if needed. That is a powerful feeling. You aren't *isolating* yourself; you're empowering yourself. Think of it this way: you know you can carry your own weight, so any support from others is an added benefit, not a crutch. This perspective frees you from fearing loneliness. You can walk into an empty room and feel at peace, not panicked, because solitude no longer equals *lonely* to you. You've proven that your happiness and stability don't depend on having others around 24/7. As a result, you can truly appreciate others' company without clinging to it. Independence has given you *freedom*. Freedom to wake up on a Saturday and decide exactly how **you** want to spend your day. Freedom to make life choices – from career moves to personal hobbies – based on your own desires, not on waiting for someone else to join you or give approval. When you're content with your own company, you live life on your terms. That autonomy is a hard-won gift you've given yourself, and it will continue to pay dividends in every aspect of your life.

Perhaps you can recall specific moments that highlight this transformation. At the start of this journey, for example, spending a Friday night alone might have felt like a failure or a punishment. Now it feels liberating – an opportunity to do whatever *you* want, be it watching your favorite show, learning a new skill, or simply enjoying the quiet. What once would have been a lonely evening is now a peaceful retreat. The difference is your mindset: you no longer equate being alone with being unwanted; you equate it with being free.

You may even find yourself doing things solo that you used to avoid – like going out to a restaurant, seeing a movie, or traveling to a new city on your own – and discovering that these experiences can be deeply fulfilling when you're confident in yourself. By embracing independence, you've opened up a whole new world of possibilities. You don't have to wait for others to live your life fully. Of course, it's wonderful to share experiences with friends or a partner, but it's equally wonderful to know you can create meaningful experiences all by yourself. This is the essence of empowerment: realizing that *your* life is in *your* hands, and that you are enough on your own. If you have a goal or dream that excites you, you can move toward it right now – no waiting for a partner or a crowd required. Climb that mountain, start that business, or write that novel if you wish, empowered by the knowledge that your own support and courage are enough to propel you forward.

Balancing Solitude with Connection

Thriving in your own company doesn't mean you *never* need or want anyone else. Human connection remains important – it's just that now you can choose companionship out of genuine desire, not out of desperation or fear of being alone. The healthiest life going forward will include a mix of quality alone time and satisfying social time. You've gained the ability to enjoy both. In fact, research shows that a balanced approach is key: too much solitude can start to hurt your well-being, just as too little solitude can leave you drained and craving space. One scientific report put it plainly: *"we may need both – time alone and time with others – in order to experience the full range of well-being benefits".* In short, you've developed a superpower (being happily alone), and now the goal is to use it wisely alongside your relationships.

How do you maintain this equilibrium? It helps to be intentional. You might establish routines that keep you socially connected while still preserving your personal space. For example, you could schedule a weekly phone call or coffee meetup with a close friend or family member – a regular touchpoint that keeps your relationships strong. At the same time, you can also block out "me time" on your calendar, perhaps a certain evening or a Sunday afternoon dedicated solely to you. Treat that appointment with yourself as non-negotiable. By structuring your week with both social plans and solo plans, you ensure neither aspect is neglected. Some people even find it helpful to literally write these into a planner: e.g., Wednesday 7–9pm: Dinner with Tom, Saturday: hiking alone in the morning. Seeing the balance in writing can remind you to honor both commitments.

Another crucial element is communicating your boundaries. Now that you know how valuable solitude is for your well-being, you can explain this to the people in your life. Let friends and family know that you cherish your time with them, but you also occasionally need personal time to recharge. True friends will understand – many may even admire this self-awareness. By being open about your needs, you prevent misunderstandings. For instance, if you decline an invite because you've had a long week and need a quiet day, the people close to you will understand that you're not pushing them away – you're simply taking care of yourself. That way, when you do engage socially, you can be fully present and upbeat.

Keeping that healthy mix of solitude and connection will guard against slipping back into either extreme of loneliness or unhealthy isolation. You won't lose yourself in others and forget to nurture your own soul, and conversely, you won't retreat so far into your own shell that you feel cut off from humanity. You've learned to walk the middle path. Even individuals who love extended solitude – like long-distance hikers who spend days alone in nature – make sure to have *intermittent social interactions* during their journeys to stay emotionally healthy. Likewise, you can enjoy your alone time knowing you have anchors in a community. When you reach out to others now, it's by choice and for mutual enrichment, not because you're lonely. And when you retreat into solitude, it's restorative, not a sign of social withdrawal. This balanced rhythm of engagement and introspection will help you continue to flourish.

Finally, remember that the "right" balance of solitude and connection is personal, and it can change with time. Some people naturally need more social interaction, while others thrive with more peaceful alone time – and both are perfectly okay. Pay attention to your own feelings as you adjust your schedule. If you notice a twinge of loneliness, that's a sign to seek out some company or reconnect with loved ones. If you start feeling overstimulated or drained, that's a cue to step back and recharge in solitude. There's truly no universal formula or "optimal" number of hours for everyone, so trust yourself to find the ratio that keeps you happy and healthy. With your new self-awareness, you can sense when you need connection and when you need quiet. By honoring those needs without guilt, you'll keep your life in balance in the way that suits *you* best.

Making Self-Care a Lifelong Habit

Over the course of this book, you've picked up a toolkit of practices to nurture your mental and emotional well-being. Now is the time to commit to making these acts of self-care a permanent part of your life. Think of all the positive habits that resonated with you – maybe you started a journal to vent and reflect, or began taking morning walks to clear your mind. Perhaps you discovered the relief of saying "no" to things that overstretch you, or the comfort of a nightly self-talk ritual where you replace negative thoughts with kinder ones. These practices are not meant to be one-off experiments. They are ongoing gifts to yourself. By consistently practicing what you've learned, you'll keep loneliness at bay and maintain the strong, content mindset you've worked so hard to build.

Self-care is a lifelong journey, not a box to check. There may be times in the future when life gets hectic or challenges arise – that's when these habits become even more crucial. For example, when you encounter stress at work or heartbreak in relationships, leaning on your self-care routines will help keep you grounded. It's all too easy under pressure to neglect ourselves, but you now know the cost of doing that. Instead, you can recognize when you're running on empty and consciously pause to recharge. Perhaps you'll notice signs of burnout and decide, "I need a weekend to myself." And you'll take it – guilt-free – because you understand that prioritizing your well-being isn't selfish, it's necessary. In fact, dedicating time to yourself nurtures a deeper understanding of who you are, which in turn leads to more authentic and meaningful connections with others. As one psychologist insightfully noted, you're not being self-indulgent when you devote regular time to yourself; you're *"being soulful"* – cultivating your inner life so that you can show up as a whole, vibrant person in the world.

So keep doing what works for you. Here are some self-care habits to make a lifelong practice:

- **Keep journaling or reflecting regularly:** Write down your thoughts and feelings on a regular basis. Journaling helps you stay in tune with yourself and track your growth. Even if it's just once a week, putting pen to paper (or fingers to keyboard) can provide insight and relieve stress.

- **Enjoy solo activities that nourish you:** Continue to spend time on pursuits that make you happy to be alone. It could be those nature walks, gardening, reading novels, crafting, or any hobby that makes you feel alive. These moments of joy in your own company will sustain you.

- **Set healthy boundaries and say "no" when needed:** Remember that it's okay to decline invitations or demands that overwhelm you. Protect your rest and energy. By saying "no" sometimes, you're saying "yes" to your well-being – and that enables you to show up better when you do say "yes."

- **Practice self-compassion and positive self-talk daily:** Keep treating yourself with kindness. If you catch your inner critic piping up, respond with a gentler voice. Remind yourself of your strengths and achievements often. Being on your own side builds an unshakable emotional foundation.

Over time, these acts of self-care will continue to yield new rewards. Perhaps your journal will become a treasure trove of insights, revealing patterns in your emotions and the progress you've made. Maybe your regular nature walks will spark fresh creative ideas or simply keep you centered through life's changes. By making self-care a permanent part of your routine, you're investing in a wiser, stronger, and more inspired version of yourself at every stage of life.

By maintaining these habits, you are essentially maintaining your relationship with yourself. You're checking in, listening, and caring – just as you would for a loved one. The relationship you have with *you* needs and deserves this attention. It's the foundation that supports all other relationships in your life.

Happiness on Your Own Terms

As we conclude our journey together, take a moment to appreciate how far you've come. You are fully capable of living a happy, fulfilling life regardless of your relationship status or social situation. This isn't just a feel-good slogan – it's a truth backed by experience and even research.

Studies have shown that getting married or finding a partner is not a guaranteed ticket to happiness. In fact, people who marry *"on average, do not become lastingly happier than they were when they were single"*. What does boost lasting happiness is living in alignment with your own values, staying true to yourself, and finding joy in everyday moments – all things you've been cultivating. You've learned to embrace who you are when you're alone, which means you carry your contentment inside you. That's a power no external circumstance can take away.

Happiness now means something personal to you. You've shed the idea that you must fit a certain mold (like always being in a relationship or constantly surrounded by friends) to be content. You have learned to write your own definition of happiness. It might be as simple as a quiet morning with coffee and a good book, feeling completely at peace. It might be pursuing a passion – painting, coding, gardening, traveling – without waiting for someone to join you, because it brings *you* joy. It might be spending time with friends on your terms, enjoying social moments without fearing solitude afterward. However you define it, your happiness is truly *yours*. You've built it from the inside out, and it reflects your unique spirit.

Take pride in the journey you've undergone. Not everyone dares to face themselves, to weather loneliness and rejection and come out stronger. But you have. Your willingness to confront the fear of loneliness head-on and turn it into personal growth is an achievement worthy of great respect. You turned moments of solitude into opportunities for growth. You stared down the feelings of loneliness and learned they were signals guiding you toward self-discovery and self-care. You put in the work – practicing self-compassion, challenging negative narratives in your head, seeking new hobbies and meaning on your own. In doing so, you've proven that you can not only be alone without feeling lonely, but actually *thrive* that way. This hard-won ability will continue to serve you for a lifetime. Whenever life brings changes – a move to a new city, a shift in friendships, a loss or a breakup – you know you'll be okay. You carry with you the confidence and grace to handle solitude, and that is immensely reassuring.

In fact, by being happy alone, you've set the stage for healthier relationships with others. Now you will seek companionship out of mutual enjoyment, not necessity. If you enter a new romance or friendship, it will be because it genuinely enriches your life – not because you fear solitude. One therapist emphasizes that *"being comfortable being alone is necessary for healthy intimate relationships,"* since individuals uncomfortable by themselves may settle for or cling to unhealthy situations. But that's no longer you. You're approaching connections from a place of wholeness, not need.

The confidence and independence you now radiate can even be magnetic. People tend to appreciate and respect those who value themselves. Don't be surprised if your self-assured solitude actually draws like-minded, positive individuals into your orbit. You're not looking for anyone to "complete" you – you are complete. This means anyone who comes into your life now is there to complement the happiness you already have, not to fix a void. In short, you can invite others in as an extension of the closeness you've cultivated with yourself. Those are exactly the kind of relationships that are genuine and fulfilling.

And on the occasional days when a pang of loneliness does resurface, remember that you have the tools to handle it. Loneliness is a normal feeling that may visit, but it no longer has power over you. You can acknowledge it and then respond in healthy ways – perhaps by reaching out to a friend or engaging in a comforting solo activity – without falling into despair. You know now that you're not truly alone; you have *you*. That knowledge will carry you through any brief lonely spells until you find your balance again.

So here you stand at the end of this book, but the beginning of a new chapter in your life – one where you are the author of your own happiness. You can face whatever comes next with a heart that is whole and open. In the years to come, you may even look back and realize that learning to be comfortable on your own was one of the greatest gifts you ever gave yourself – a gift that will continue to enrich your life. If you find love or deepen old friendships, it will be because you want to, not because you need to. If you spend stretches of time on your own, you will enjoy your own company and use it for reflection and renewal. In truth, you'll probably have the best of both worlds: love and connection flowing in and out of your life, while the steady glow of your inner contentment remains. Remember to celebrate yourself – not just today, as you close this chapter, but every day that you choose to live by the lessons you've learned. You know now how to be alone without feeling lonely, and with that knowledge comes a profound peace. Carry it forward into your fulfilling life ahead, and embrace the freedom, balance, self-love, and happiness that are now yours to enjoy.

Epilogue

You have traveled far since opening this book. The person who first picked up these pages—perhaps hesitant, maybe even skeptical—has transformed into someone who understands that solitude can be sanctuary, that rejection can be redirection, and that the most reliable companion you'll ever have lives within you.

The tools you've gathered here aren't meant to gather dust on mental shelves. They require practice, patience, and gentle persistence. Some days, your inner voice will sound like your dearest friend. Other days, that voice might need coaching back to kindness. Both experiences are normal, both are part of the beautiful, messy process of becoming whole.

Remember that choosing solitude differs entirely from having loneliness thrust upon you. The former represents power; the latter, circumstance. You now possess the ability to transform any circumstance into an opportunity for growth, reflection, and self-discovery. When rejection comes knocking—and it will—you can greet it with curiosity rather than devastation. What lesson does this carry? What new direction might this open?

Your relationship with yourself sets the template for every other relationship in your life. By learning to enjoy your own company, you've raised the standard for how others must treat you. By developing mental resilience, you've created an unshakeable foundation that external storms cannot destroy.

The journey continues beyond these final words. Each quiet morning, every solo meal, all those moments when you choose your own company over settling for poor company—these become victories. You've learned that being alone doesn't mean being left behind; sometimes, you're simply arriving early to your own life.

Step forward with confidence. Your most extraordinary adventures are just beginning, and you're finally ready to enjoy them fully—starting with the remarkable person you've become.

www.ingramcontent.com/pod-product-compliance
Lightning Source LLC
Chambersburg PA
CBHW071515120626
46550CB00006B/2233